Washington and Vietnam

"Powerful and rich beyond all ken . . .
Swearing vengeance, proclaiming duty,
we heap offerings on the pyre and hope
the gods of history will judge us kind-
ly." Max Frankel, in a review of *Vietnam Witness: 1953-1966*, by Bernard B.
Fall. *New York Times Book Review*,
May 22, 1966

*For Sandy and Richard and all
my young fellow Americans*

WASHINGTON
and
VIETNAM

An examination of the
Moral and Political Issues

by DOROTHY DUNBAR BROMLEY

1966

Oceana Publications, Inc.
Dobbs Ferry, N.Y.

Acknowledgments

In the course of research that was as wide-ranging as it was arduous, the author found of invaluable assistance Bernard B. Fall's *The Two Vietnams* (Praeger, 1963, rev. 1964), and his *Vietnam Witness: 1953-1966,* (Praeger, 1966), as well as his other writings.

Vietnam—History, Documents, and Opinions on a Major World Crisis, the paperback "reader" edited by Marvin E. Gettleman (Fawcett, 1965) was an indispensable source.

From Jean Lacouture's *Vietnam: Between Two Truces* (Random, 1966) and his article, "Turning Point in Vietnam," published in the March 3, 1966 issue of *The New York Review of Books,* illuminating insights were gained.

Among American observers on the scene, the objective reports of Charles Mohr, Neil Sheehan and R. W. Apple, Jr., of the *New York Times'* Saigon Bureau, provided a rich mine of information.

To other correspondents and scholars whose reports and studies have been drawn upon, the author owes a debt of thanks.

She is deeply grateful to Dr. John C. Bennett and the Committee of Clergy and Laymen Concerned About Vietnam for their encouragement of her labours and their sponsorship of the end result. For editing the manuscript, she thanks Philip Scharper, a co-chairman of the Committee.

Professor Gettleman was so kind as to screen the manuscript for historical accuracy and to suggest a sharper forcus for Chapter I.

The literate interest of Julie Lockard, Darnell Rudd and Lindsay Stewart, who typed portions of the manuscript, sustained the author's morale. At the Committee office, Richard Fernandez and Sandy Whiteley were an ever-present help.

D.D.B.

Contents

34812

Note to the Reader

"Our fighting men are in Vietnam," President Johnson told a New York audience on February 23, 1966, "because tens of thousands of invaders came south before them. Our numbers have increased in Vietnam because the aggression of others has increased . . . The high hopes of the aggressor have been dimmed, and the tide of the battle has been turned."

On other occasions the President has said we make war only to assure to the South Vietnamese people "the essential rights of human existence" and to "defend the free world" against the advance of Communism.

His rhetoric has not persuaded all of the American people. A growing body of opinion holds that by waging this war to contain Communism, a war never declared by Congress, our Government is in fact encouraging the spread of Communism, is martyrizing the Vietnamese people, and risking a confrontation with China that could lead to a nuclear holocaust.

Ranged between the President's sharp critics at one end of the spectrum, and, at the other, those Americans who believe with him that Communism can and must be checked in Southeast Asia, no matter how great the cost in American lives and treasure, are many other Americans who are perplexed and troubled. They ask: Do the Vietnamese people themselves want the war to go on or do they wish we would leave? Is it a war of aggression or a civil war? If we are winning, why must we send more and more troops? What are the dangers of escalation? Why have all attempts at negotiations failed?

To help fellow citizens make up their own minds about the rightness or wrongness of the course our Government is pursuing, this condensed study seeks to set forth objective facts and dispassionate judgments.

D.D.B.

New York City
July 22, 1966

In Lieu of a
Declaration of War

He had never been known as "the great dissenter." Never before had J. William Fulbright of Arkansas, Chairman of the Senate's Foreign Relations Committee since 1959, challenged the policy of a Democratic President.

Our escalating war in Vietnam had become for him a crisis of conscience, a crisis, as he saw it, for his Committee and the entire Senate, which had allowed its constitutional powers of advice and consent to atrophy—as he said in his first Johns Hopkins lecture on April 21, 1966— "into what is widely regarded . . . to be a duty to give prompt consent with a minimum of advice. . . ."

To underscore the Senate's constitutional powers and to educate the American public, Mr. Fulbright broke precedent. He held open Committee hearings on this country's involvement in Vietnam—and invited in the TV cameras. During the first two weeks of those hearings in February, what the senators themselves said—the voicing of deep anxiety around the table, the hard look at Administration policy taken by a courageous minority— had as great an impact on TV viewers as the testimony of the Committee's witnesses—distinguished critics of President Johnson and his own top spokesmen.

Speaking for himself, Sen. Fulbright admitted past errors of omission and commission as Chairman of a Committee that had been insufficiently vigilant. A few weeks earlier, on the CBS Reports program broadcast February 1, he had made a notable confession. Had the Presidential campaign not been underway in August, 1964, and had he not been so strongly opposed to Barry Goldwater, Mr. Fulbright admitted, he would not have pushed through the resolution which President Johnson has since interpreted as authorizing him to carry on full-scale military operations in Vietnam.

President Johnson had asked for the joint resolution after two United States destroyers were attacked, on July 31, 1964, by North Vietnamese torpedo boats in the Gulf of Tonkin and our bombers had made heavy reprisal raids. The resolution put Congress on record as supporting — until such time as it might choose to rescind the legislation — "the determination of the President, as Commander-in-Chief, to take all necessary measures to repel any armed attack against the forces of the United States and to prevent further aggression."

"The United States," the resolution read, "regards as vital to its national interest and to world peace the maintenance of international peace and security in Southeast Asia. Consonant with the Constitution . . . and the Charter of the United Nations and in accordance with its obligations under the Southeast Asia Collective Defense Treaty, the United States is, therefore, prepared as the President determines, to take all necessary steps, including the use of armed force, to assist any member or protocol state . . . requesting assistance in defense of its freedom."

Eighteen months later Mr. Fulbright considered the Tonkin Gulf Resolution a grave mistake. Deploring the Administration's resumption of bombing of North Vietnam after the 37-day pause, Mr. Fulbright told CBS' Eric Sevareid and Martin Agronsky:

I have played a part . . . that I am not at all proud of . . . I should have had greater foresight . . . That would have been a good time to have precipitated a debate and a reexamination . . . of our involvement . . . it was during . . . the beginning of the presidential campaign. I was very much a partisan . . . for Johnson . . . I disapproved of the statements of Mr. Goldwater and I went along with the urging, I may say, of the Administration. I think it is a terrible situation we are in. I am hoping we can find an honorable way out of it.

Sen. Fulbright's reference to the Presidential campaign implied that the Administration had felt it needed the resolution to counter Goldwater's charge that the

President was pursuing a no-win policy in Vietnam. Walking a tight-rope, President Johnson voiced his firm determination to contain Communism in Southeast Asia, ·but assured his fellow countrymen he would follow no such reckless course as was being urged by Goldwater, who, many voters feared, might resort to nuclear warfare were he elected.

"They call upon us," President Johnson said in a speech on August 12, 1964, "to supply American boys to do the job that Asian boys should do. They ask us to take reckless action that might risk the lives of millions . . . and threaten the peace of the entire world." As the President spoke, less than a week after the stiff Gulf of Tonkin resolution had been passed, our forces in Vietnam were about to be increased to 25,000 and "advisers" were being killed or wounded in combat operations.

In early August, 1964, the public's chief worry was over whether our reprisal raids on North Vietnam's torpedo boat bases would trigger Communist China's entry into the war. When Peking did not react, Americans drew a long breath of relief, and were mostly unaware of the grave import of the resolution which had been passed.

In the Senate, Oregon's Wayne Morse pointed out that the presence of our destroyers in the Gulf of Tonkin at a time when South Vietnamese ships of American origin were shelling islands off the coast of North Vietnam, "was bound to be looked upon by our enemies as an act of provocation." When Sen. Nelson, D., of Wisconsin enquired how close to shore our ships had been patrolling, Mr. Fulbright, who had been secretly briefed by Secretary of Defense McNamara, admitted that we had gone in "at least 11 miles . . . to show that we do not recognize {North Vietnam's} 12-mile limit." But in reply to a question from Sen. Ellender, D., of Louisiana, Mr. Fulbright said our destroyers "had no connection whatever with any ships that might have been operating in the area."

Kentucky's Senator John Sherman Cooper, R., asked whether Congress was giving Mr. Johnson "advance authority to take whatever action he may deem necessary respecting South Vietnam" even if that "could lead us into war." Mr. Fulbright replied, "That is the way I would interpret it." Maryland's Senator Brewster, D., declared he "would look with great dismay" if the U.S. landed armies on the Asian continent. Senator Nelson offered an amendment adding the words: "except when provoked to a greater response, we should continue to attempt to avoid a direct military involvement in the Southeast Asia conflict." As the Administration's spokesman, Mr. Fulbright refused to accept the Nelson amendment—and regrets today that he brushed it off.

The Gulf of Tonkin resolution was passed by the Senate, with only the two Democrats, Morse, and Gruening, of Alaska, dissenting. In the House, the vote was unanimous.

Mr. Fulbright's vigorous sponsorship in 1964 of the Gulf of Tonkin resolution was in sharp contrast to his strong objections in 1955 to a similar resolution—one concerning Taiwan, where Chiang Kai Shek had established his Republic of China after being driven from the mainland in 1949 by the Chinese Communists. As devised by Secretary of State Dulles, the Taiwan resolution expressed Congressional support for actions taken not only in defense of Taiwan but "such related positions" as "are now in friendly hands"—meaning the islands of Quemoy and Matsu off the Chinese coast, held by Chiang. At that time Mr. Fulbright and Hubert Humphrey, then a senator, declared Mr. Dulles' refusal to consider any modification of the resolution deprived the Senate of its constitutional right to "advise" and left it only with the right "to consent." In those days Mr. Fulbright, a Democrat, opposed a foreign policy maneuver of a Republican administration. Today he and other leading Democrats are critical of their own President.

When, late in January, 1966, Sen. Hartke of Indiana and fourteen other Democratic senators wrote Mr. Johnson urging that the bombing pause be continued, the President in a short letter said he continued "to be guided in these matters by the resolution of the Congress, approved on August 10, 1964." A few days later the Senate Foreign Relations Committee announced it would hold open hearings on our involvement in Vietnam.

During the hearings, Sen. Morse drove home the point that only Congress, under Art. I, Sect. 8, Clause

11 of the Constitution, has the power to declare war. "It will not be too long," he predicted, "before the American people repudiate our war in Southeast Asia."

Tennessee's Senator Albert Gore, D., commented that, as the war widened, most members of Congress were almost as much in the dark as the public. Because of the threat of nuclear war, Mr. Gore declared, the Committee should have held hearings three years ago, and pleaded guilty to not having in past months shared his misgivings with the public. It seemed to him that the commitment of U.S. combat forces was "a serious mistake that has increased, rather than diminished, the danger of a major war."

Idaho's Sen. Church, D., pointed out that we still have 55,000 troops in South Korea and said, "We must not permit South Vietnam to become another Asian garrison for American forces."

Sen. Gruening charged, "We are being led more and more deeply into a war in which Congress has no real voice."

Sen. Case, R., of New Jersey said he did not regard his vote for the Gulf of Tonkin resolution as meaning he had abdicated his responsibility and given the President "a completely free rein."

"We are involved," Sen. McGovern, D. of South Dakota, said on the Senate floor, "in what I believe is the most dangerous venture in which this country has ever engaged. We must turn every possible stone . . . to end this war . . . before we are pulled into what could be the most disastrous development anyone could imagine . . . a major all-out war on the Asian mainland."

In a classic exchange with Secretary Rusk during the hearings, Sen. Fulbright declared,

> There must be something wrong with our diplomacy . . . How can you expect any development in any direction when we . . . have taken such an adamant attitude . . . I get the impression . . . the only kind of settlement is unconditional surrender . . . we are the strongest nation in the world. We can probably impose our will. I am saying that this is not wise in the long run. . . .

At the other end of the Committee spectrum, Missouri's Senator Stuart Symington, D., held that Red China is "a serious menace" to us today, and that in North Vietnam we must more effectively use our superior air and sea power to contain Communism in Southeast Asia. Holding the same view, Louisiana's Russell Long, D., declared in a floor speech he had information from "very high sources" that the Communist cause was being aided by speeches of critical senators.

While the consensus on the Committee was that we should not at this juncture pull out our forces from South Vietnam, a majority of the worried members showed great interest in Gen. Gavin's proposal, endorsed by Mr. Kennan, that we limit our military objectives and defend only selected strategic areas in South Vietnam.

Of the thirteen Democrats on the Committee, seven made it clear they deplored the widening of the war in Vietnam and feared the results of further escalation. If they regretted having voted for the Gulf of Tonkin resolution, there seemed little chance they would as a group go along with Sen. Morse on a vote for rescinding it, at a time when we were at war in Southeast Asia.

On March 1, Mr. Morse introduced his repealer in the form of an amendment to the $4.8 billion bill to provide additional funds for the Vietnamese war. In a parliamentary maneuver, Majority Leader Mansfield of Montana—who had been absent from the hearings because of illness—made a non-debatable motion to table Mr. Morse's amendment. The vote on tabling was something less than an overwhelming victory for President Johnson. Negative votes were cast not only, as expected, by Morse and Gruening, but by Sen. Fulbright, and two other well-known Democrats, Eugene McCarthy of Minnesota, and Young of Ohio.

When the defense approporation bill, minus the Morse amendment, came to a vote, only Morse and Gruening voted against it. The general feeling was that necessary supplies must be provided for our fighting men in Vietnam.

The successful tabling motion—the President's strong supporters in the Senate claimed—was in effect a reaffirmation of the controversial 1964 resolution. But his critics rose to object to such an interpretation.

6

In the House, the military appropriations bill was passed by a vote of 392-4. Voting "no" were Burton and Brown of California, Ryan of Manhattan, and Conyers of Michigan, all Democrats.

"The Senate as a whole," Mr. Fulbright told his Johns Hopkins audience, ". . . should undertake to revive and strengthen the deliberative function which it has permitted to atrophy in the course of 25 years of crisis. Acting on the premise that dissent is not disloyalty, that a true consensus is shaped by airing our differences rather than suppressing them, the Senate should again become, as it used to be, an institution in which the great issues of American politics are contested with thoroughness, energy and candor.

Nor should the Senate allow itself to be too easily swayed by executive pleas for urgency and un-animity, or by allegations of aid and comfort to the enemies of the United States made by of-ficials whose concern may be heightened by a distaste for criticism directed at themselves.

"Some of our superpatriots assume that any war the United States fights is a just war, if not indeed a holy crusade, but history does not sustain their view. . . . In an historical frame of reference it seems to me logical and proper to question the wisdom of our present military involvement in Asia. . . ."

Brushing off the Senate's constitutional prerogatives, and his own duty to consult it on foreign policy, Mr. Johnson declared in his July 1st Omaha speech, the day after he had escalated the war by bombing North Viet-nam's large oil tanks near Hanoi and Haiphong: "Now there are many, many, many who can recommend and ad-vise and sometimes a few consent. But there is only one who has been chosen by the American people to decide . . . . Twenty months ago, in a great national election . . . the people of 44 states of this Union . . . gave me a direction and voted me a majority for the Presidency of this country. . . ."

The *N.Y. Times'* White House correspondent, Tom Wicker, commented:

It would be hard to interpret the 1964 election {landslide} as a mandate for recent American actions in Vietnam. Then, it was Barry Goldwater who urged bombing supply lines, "strong affirmative action" and carrying the war to the North. It was Mr. Johnson who said in 1964 that "we are not going North and we are not going South" . . . . He said the cause of freedom was not advanced "by calling on the full might of our military to solve every problem." He called enlargement of the war "reckless."

Vietnam's present can only be understood in terms of its past. During the first millenium of the Christian era, the ethnic Viets, who then inhabited only the Red River Delta of Tonkin centering around Hanoi, chafed under and periodically revolted against Chinese domination. The Chinese brought Buddhism, along with Confucianism and Taoism; and their cultural influence was to persist after they were driven out in 939 AD. Yet the Vietnamese kept their national identity, having their own language, literature and folklore. Once they were free of the Chinese, the vigorous Vietnamese pushed south along the coastal plain in search of rice-lands to feed their growing population. They overcame the now extinct Chams in the area known as Assam, which is split today between the North and South Zones, but whose main cities, Danang and Hué, are in South Vietnam. Moving still farther south, the Vietnamese colonized the Mekong Delta, and by 1802 had dislodged the Khmer-Cambodians from what came to be known as Cochin-China, with Saigon as its capital. This was the first area to be conquered in 1862, by the French, who made it a colony, exerting there a greater cultural and political influence than in Tonkin and Assam, which several decades later came under French rule as protectorates.

Western conquest and geography had divided Vietnam, like all Gaul, into three parts. As descendants of the ethnic Vietnamese, the hard-working Tonkinese of North Vietnam are still inclined, George A. Carver, Jr. wrote in the Apr. 1965 issue of *Foreign Affairs*, "to think of themselves as the natural leaders of all Vietnam, an attitude resented by both Annamite and Cochin-Chinese." Cliques representing the three regimes "exist in every politically significant group," exercising "a jealous watchfulness over the regional balances struck with regard to advantage, preferment and influence."

Cutting across the regional jealousies is the centuries-old rift between Buddhists and Catholics. Jesuit missionaries began their proselytizing in the 16th century and from the first the Buddhists, always strong nationalists, sought to prevent the spread of Christianity, "a foreign doctrine." But the Jesuits made their converts and opened the way to French political encroachment. The Vietnamese Catholics, a mandarin at the Hué court was to say, served as the claws which enabled the French crab to crawl across the land. In the mid-19th century, the xenophobic Emperor Tu Duc launched a program against the missionaries and their flocks, instilling fear of persecution in future generations of Catholics.

After the French seized the country, resistance to colonial rule was always under the surface, at times openly led by Vietnamese mandarins. By the 1920's an underground Nationalist Party comprised diverse elements. With the rise of the Indochinese Communist Party, resistance to the French came to be spearheaded by Ho Chi Minh. In the year 1930 a peasant revolt was brutally put down by the French, who threw 10,000 into prison and executed many Communist leaders. As an official of the Far Eastern Bureau of the Comintern, Ho was arrested and imprisoned in 1931 in Hong Kong by the British.

The well-educated, Moscow-trained Ho, who was destined to be worshipped in Southeast Asia as a revolutionary hero, was born into a family of some distinction in 1890 in a village in Annam where, as a boy of 12, he carried conspiratorial messages for his elders. His family name was Nguyen, later discarded for his pseudonym, which means "He who Enlightens." In the 1920's, when he was living in France, Ho had joined the Party there and had soon become a leader in the Communist struggle against colonialism. At that time he called himself Nguyen Ai Quoc, meaning "Cho, the Patriot," to show that he believed nationalism compatible with Communism.

During World War II, Communist guerrillas and a variety of activist nationalists harried the Japanese occupation forces and their French collaborators. As members of the League for the Independence of Vietnam, they were known as the Vietminh; they became a force to be reckoned with after Ho, who had been serving another prison term, this time in China, had been released by Chiang Kai Shek in 1943. During the last six months of World War II, Ho and his followers—with the help of our Army's Office of Strategic Services, forerunner of the Central Intelligence Agency—cleared the Japanese out of extensive areas in the northernmost provinces. On the heels of the Japanese defeat, Ho marched into Hanoi, the northern capitol, to the cheers of the populace. On September 2, 1945, he proclaimed the Democratic Republic of Vietnam.

The new republic's constitution (since revised) echoed our Declaration of Independence: "All men are created equal . . ." "We are convinced," the document read, "that the Allies who recognized the principles of equality at the conferences of Tehran and San Francisco cannot fail to recognize the independence of Vietnam." It was an optimistic assumption. Ho Chi Minh's regime did establish itself in the North, where Chiang's Chinese troops, who had been delegated by the Big Three at Potsdam to supercede the Japanese north of the 16th parallel, were tolerant of the new state and themselves stayed only four months.

The story was different in the South, where the new regime held power in Saigon for only a month. It was ousted by the British, who had been delegated at Potsdam to take over from the Japanese. Shortly thereafter, the French, at the invitation of the British, sent in fresh military forces which were to remain for nine more years.

Yet in March, 1946, France recognized Ho's republic as a free, but not independent, state within the French Union and the Indochinese Federation, consisting of Vietnam, Laos, and Cambodia. In September, Ho signed in Paris a *modus vivendi*, which did not, however, cover Cochin-China, the southernmost part of the country. In any event the accord was breached in November when the French, insisting upon customs control, bombed Haiphong from the harbor, killing thousands of Vietnamese. By 1946 the French were under attack in both north and south. The Indochinese war had begun, although it was to accelerate slowly.

In the first stage of the war, from '46 to '48, the French openly tried to reimpose colonial rule. In the second stage, they claimed they were defending Vietnamese nationalism in the person of the Emperor Bao Dai, who had abdicated when Ho Chi Minh formed the new republic. The French restored the emperor to power, to rule over a new political entity, the State of Vietnam.

The French maneuver did not wholly succeed. By 1949 the Vietminh had occupied more than half of the countryside. Their guerrilla forces included besides the hard-core Communists, who exercized military and political leadership, various nationalists and members of the Democratic and Socialist parties who held seats in Ho's cabinet. Claiming 9 million members, the Vietminh set up "national welfare" groups of women, youth, workers, peasants and soldiers. Underestimating the enemy, French officers called them "*les jaunes*"—"the yellow ones." Later, American officers were to dismiss the Vietcong, a UPI correspondent reported, as "raggedy little bastards in black pajamas."

In the early years of the war against the French, the Vietminh leaders actually hoped for American aid—on the theory that our government would seek to extend its influence in Southeast Asia by supporting the Vietnamese people's fight against the old imperialist system. President Roosevelt was against French colonialism and had wanted Vietnam to become a mandated territory once the United Nations was created. But in 1950 the French elevated the war to a third stage, calling it purely and simply a war against Communism. President Truman and Secretary of State Acheson were quick to see it in this light, and we were soon providing the French with planes and military advisers and supplies. Before the end of the war we were meeting 80% of the French war costs.

The surrender by the French, on May 7, 1954, of the jungle fortress at Dienbienphu in the far north, marked the end of an epoch. "The Asians, after centuries of subjugation," the Southeast Asian scholar, Bernard B. Fall has written, "had beaten the white man at his own game." The accord signed at Geneva on July 21 provided: that Vietnam be provisionally divided at the 17th parallel, pending elections to be held in 1956; that the opposing armed forces be regrouped, the Vietminh to withdraw to the north and the French to the South, where they were to remain until the July, 1956 elections were held. It was agreed further that neither party would make a military alliance nor permit the construction of a military base under foreign control, and that there be no increment of military supplies and personnel in either Zone. The estimated 600 American advisers and technicians who had been assigned to the French were to be allowed to remain in the Southern Zone.

The victory over the French heightened the prestige of Ho Chi Minh and General Vo Nguyen Giap. Yet many people in the Southern Zone complained they had fought the French only to have Ho agree to provisional partition.

III
Truman and Eisenhower Commitments

President Truman in 1947 laid down the doctrine that the United States would "help free peoples to maintain . . . their national integrity against aggressive movements that seek to impose upon them totalitarian regimes." Under this doctrine, Washington in the postwar years helped the Greek Government put down insurgency and thus "contain Communism." The new policy, devised for Europe, was to be extended to Asia.

In China we had placed all of our bets on Chiang and his warlords—and lost in 1949 when he was driven from the mainland by the Chinese Communists. When the North Korean Communists, in June 1950, invaded South Korea, President Truman got quick support for United Nations "police action," in the absence from the Security Council of the U.S.S.R. The Korean War had started and the United States was to the end to provide the bulk of the UN forces.

The Truman administration was as wary of the Vietminh as of the Korean Communists. When, early in 1950, Ho Chi Minh asked other countries to recognize the Democratic Republic of Vietnam, Communist China and the U.S.S.R. promptly did so. Ho was now revealed, Secretary of State Dean Acheson declared, "in his true colors as the mortal enemy of native independence in Indo-china." The year before, the Department of State had welcomed the formation of "Bao Dai's new unified state." In May 1950, Mr. Acheson announced that the U.S. would grant military and economic aid to the three states of Indochina and to France in order to restore security and develop "genuine nationalism." A month later, after the outbreak of the Korean War, President Truman said our aid to Indochina would be accelerated, and dispatched a military mission to Saigon.

The American determination to contain Communism in Asia lost none of its momentum under President Eisenhower's Secretary of State, John Foster Dulles. Eisenhower himself urged upon Churchill a coalition of forces to support the French in the Indochinese War, as he recalls in his memoirs, *Mandate for Change.*" If Indochina," he wrote Churchill, on April 4, 1954, "passes into the hands of the Communists, the ultimate effect of your and our global strategic position . . . could be disastrous."

There is fairly strong evidence that in the last stage of the Indochinese War, Mr. Dulles pushed for American military intervention to save the French. On June 7, 1954, Chalmers Roberts of the *Washington Post and Times-Herald,* published an account, amplified in *The Reporter* of September 14, 1954, of how Dulles had, on April 3, summoned to an emergency conference with himself and Admiral Arthur W. Radford, Chairman of the Joint Chiefs of Staff, the Congressional leaders of both parties. Dienbinephu could be saved, they were told, if U.S. planes from Navy carriers then in the China sea and others from the Philippines were to make a strike. This was at a time when the French and the Vietminh had already agreed to hold peace talks in Geneva. President Eisenhower had gone off to the country but had told Dulles such a move would have to be first authorized by a Joint Resolution of Congress. The party leaders, among them Lyndon B. Johnson, then Democratic leader of the Senate, said they would go along with Dulles' intervention only if he could round up allies. The Secretary tried, but was stopped in his course by Anthony Eden and Churchill's cabinet.

Mr. Johnson was reported to have said at the time he was "against sending GI's into the mud and muck of Indochina on a blood-letting spree to perpetuate colonialism and the white man's exploitation of Asia."

Mr. Roberts' story was denied on the floor of the Senate on July 9, 1954, by Republicans Homer Ferguson and Alexander Smith. And in a press conference held January 13, 1960, President Eisenhower declared "there was never any plan developed to put into execution in Indochina." Yet an account of the incident published by James Shepley in *Life,* January 16, 1956, was said by Dulles at a subsequent press conference "not to require correction."

15

Only when government documents become available will it be known whether Eisenhower was ready to approve, given Congress' consent, military intervention in a situation that, he was to write later in *Mandate for Change,* seemed hopeless. There he wrote, "The enemy {the Vietminh} had much popular sympathy, and many civilians aided them by providing both shelter and information. . . ."

"I have never talked or corresponded," Eisenhower wrote, "with a person knowledgeable in Indochinese affairs who did not agree that had elections been held as of the time of the fighting, possibly 80% of the populace would have voted for the Communist Ho Chi Minh . . . rather than Chief of State Bao Dai. . . ."

Short of supplying combat forces, the U.S. had done everything possible to encourage the French to continue fighting the Vietminh and so contain Communism. The French felt the impact when we signed a truce with the North Koreans in July, 1953—Eisenhower having promised in his campaign that he would end the unpopular war. Now China, which had sent military supplies and volunteers to help the North Koreans, could provide the Vietminh with the artillery and ammunition which turned the tide at Dienbienphu.

When the French collapsed, the U.S. had to countenance the Geneva settlement, which left the Communists in control of North Vietnam. As a line of defense against further encroachment, Secretary Dulles created the Southeast Asia Treaty Organization for collective defense. The treaty was signed in Sept., 1954, by the U.S., the United Kingdom, and France; and by Pakistan, Thailand, the Philippines, Australia and New Zealand, but not by India, Japan and Burma, three leading nations that have a geographical interest in Southeast Asia.

In South Vietnam, the U.S. hoped that a strong leader might be found who would offer the people an attractive alternative to Ho Chi Minh's Communist program.

IV
Diem, the Man
of the Hour

Ngo Dinh Diem, a man of stature who was as strong a nationalist as an anti-Communist, seemed to be the answer to American prayers. He came of a Vietnamese mandarin family in Assam that had converted to Catholicism in the 17th Century, a feudal family that had ruled through the French. Diem favored neither the French nor Japanese during World War II. But neither did he line up with the Vietminh, then or during the First Indochinese War. Diem considered himself a man of destiny and to further his ambition came to the United States in 1950 at the invitation of Wesley Fishel, later a professor of political science at Michigan State University. During his first and subsequent visits in the next three years, Diem came to know and be admired by Cardinal Spellman, Supreme Court Justice William O. Douglas and Senators Mike Mansfield and John F. Kennedy. In Washington, during the McCarthy period, Diem's strong anti-Communism favorably impressed the Eisenhower administration.

The lightning struck for Diem when he was in Paris in June, 1954, while the Geneva talks were under way. Bao Dai, who was also there, made him premier of the shreds of his French-supported regime and granted Diem the dictatorial powers he demanded.

Four months later, on October 24, President Eisenhower wrote Diem in Saigon, offering American aid, "to assist the Government of Vietnam in developing and maintaining a strong, viable state, capable of resisting attempted subversion or aggression through military means." There was fear of aggression from the Northern Zone and of subversion from the Vietminh who had remained in the Southern Zone.

Eisenhower has since said he never promised to send combat troops. Yet it is this "commitment" to the South Vietnamese people to which President Johnson has so frequently referred. His critics point out that Washington's backing of Diem had more than a little to do with his rise to power; we had in fact merely made a commitment to ourselves. The offer was conditioned upon Diem's "standards of performance" in undertaking "needed reforms." Yet within four months, a U.S. Military Advisory Group took over the training of the South Vietnamese Army.

Diem moved quickly to consolidate his power. He ousted Bao Dai's Army Chief of Staff; placed members of his family in key posts, and drove into hiding the Cao-Dai, the Buddhist Hoa-Hao, and other armed sects.

In mid-1955, Diem refused to meet with leaders from the North to plan for the reunification election scheduled, by the Geneva accords, for the summer of 1956. Instead, he held in South Vietnam in October of that year a referendum which, by a 98% vote, ousted Bao Dai and made Diem the Zone's absolute ruler. Diem's referendum—in the view of a senior political adviser at the British Embassy—was conducted "with a cynical disregard for decency and democratic principles."

There was no popular outcry when the elections were scuttled. Ho Chi Minh had lost some of his popularity among non-Communists in the South, as a result of North Vietnam's Chinese-type agrarian reform program, which brought on a peasant rebellion. It was brutally put down and some 50,000 killed. Later Gen. Giap confessed in print that "errors" had been committed.

From the start, Ho's regime was feared by many of the Catholic minority in South Vietnam, including the 700,000 refugees who had fled South. They looked to Diem as their protector. A strong Catholic himself, Diem placed Catholics in key positions, used them as his shock troops, and showed such favoritism as to outrage the Buddhists, who constitute most of South Vietnam's population.

Diem, too, had a "land reform" program. The old system, which had been abolished by the Vietminh, who allowed tenants to till the land without paying rent or taxes, was restored. Taxes were reimposed and back rents were collected for landlords who had fled during the war against the French. Peasants were uprooted to make way for the Catholic refugees from the North. Many of the latter were settled in a ring around Saigon as a protection for the Diem regime.

In the United States, Diem was praised for his administrative genius.

In May, 1957, he enjoyed a triumphal visit to this country. He was met at the airport by President Eisenhower, addressed a joint session of Congress and was given a dinner in New York by the American Friends of Vietnam, which had senators and liberals on its letterhead. Diem received the Richard E. Byrd award for "inspired leadership in the cause of the free world," and was described in a *N.Y. Times* editorial as "a man of deep religious heart," a man with "a firm concept of human rights," with whom "Thomas Jefferson would have no quarrel."

Life took a different line. Its lay-out of May 13, 1957 was captioned "The Tough Miracle Man of Vietnam." "Behind a facade of photographs, flags and slogans," the text of the article read, "there is a grim structure of decrees, 're-education' centers, secret police. Presidential 'Ordinance No. 6' signed and issued by Diem provides that 'individuals considered dangerous to national defense . . . may be confined on 'executive order' in a 'concentration camp' . . . many non-communists have . . . been detained. . . .''

But *Life* thought the ends justified the means. "Ngo Dinh Diem," the magazine pointed out, "is respected in Vietnam today for the miracles he has wrought. . . . To a world daunted by the idea that circumstances are bigger than men, one man with a purpose is demonstrating what he calls 'the power of human personality'."

Describing Diem's use of informers and tough "mopping-up operations," the French scholar and long-time resident of Vietnam, Philippe Devillers, writes: "The repression affected all those, and they were many—Democrats, Socialists, liberals, adherents of the sects—who were bold enough to express their disagreement. . . . It soon became evident to many Western observers that {Diem's} policy was playing into the hands of the Communists. . . . There were denunciations, encirclement of villages, searches and raids, . . . plundering, interrogations, enlivened sometimes by torture (even of innocent people) . . ." There was reason to suspect, the French scholar added, that the repressions were "encouraged by certain American activists."[*]

The American advisers who were reportedly closest to Diem were the members of the Michigan State University Group which had been sent to Vietnam in 1955 by the Eisenhower Administration to advise on government reorganization and the retraining of the national police force, with aid from the CIA. Head of the group was Prof. Wesley Fishel, who had started Diem on his way to the United States.

So great was Prof. Fishel's confidence in Diem that he wrote for the *New Leader* of November 2, 1959, an article captioned "Vietnam's Democratic One-Man Rule." "No one," Mr. Fishel asserted, "who has known Ngo Dinh Diem can fail to be impressed by his determination to . . . bring increasing benefits, happiness, and freedoms to his countrymen. . . . It may seem paradoxical to some that out of strong governmental power may come individual freedom. But considering the context in which Vietnam exists, can one think of a more dependable method of assuring it?"

The South Vietnamese villagers had no "freedom" under Diem, and suffered from mounting repressions. In the early years, in the South, the Vietminh had stayed quiet, counting on the Geneva-mandated reunification elections which were never held, and then, hopefully, on counter-measures from Ho Chi Minh's regime. But only diplomatic notes of protest came from Hanoi and from the U.S.S.R., whose Foreign Minister had presided as co-chairman at the Geneva Conference.

Finally, in 1958, the Vietminh went into action. Appealing to the villagers who had been alienated by the Diem regime, it organized the Veterans of the Resistance. With home-made weapons and arms kept since 1954, the veterans captured village after village. Perjoratively, Diem's forces called all of the resisters, Vietcong, meaning Viet-

---

[*]Philippe, Devillers. *The China Quarterly* (London), Jan.-Mch., '62

Communists.* The Government forces had superior American arms, planes and helicopters, but had neither the skill of the experienced guerrillas nor the support of the populace. They failed to recapture the lost villages. "Vietnam is a nation at war," Diem admitted to a French correspondent in 1959. The miracle had been short-lived.

By 1960, *Life* found Diem no longer "a national hero;" *Time* commented: "Pleading the Communist threat, Diem has ruled with rigged elections, a muzzled press and political 're-education camps' that now hold 30,000."

To thwart the guerrillas, Diem had his forces build "strategic hamlets"—fortified enclosures into which whole villages were herded. The aim was to deprive the Vietcong—Mao's proverbial revolutionary "fish"—of the "water" in which they lived, moved and fed.

In 1959, Diem promulgated a new law which called for the "repression of acts of sabotage, of infringements of national security, and of attacks upon the life or property of citizens." Military tribunals sentenced the accused to death or life imprisonment and no appeal was allowed. The persecutions helped bring on the Vietcong rebellion.

In November, 1960, a military coup against Diem failed—perhaps because the American Ambassador had reportedly said American funds would go only to a regime headed by Diem. The coup was led by a young colonel of the Buddhist faith, Nguyn Chanh Thi, the same officer, later a Lt. General, whose ouster in March, 1966, from Premier Nugyen Cao Ky's military directorate, precipitated the militant Buddhists' move against Ky.

By 1962, Robert Shaplen wrote in *The Lost Revolution*, some 20,000 political prisoners were held in about fifty jails. He reported:

> Many were captured Vietcong insurgents, but there were also a lot of "suspects" who had languished in jails for months or even years . . . {including} some 300 non-Communist liberals arrested solely for having expressed anti-Diem views or for being suspected of having spoken out in favor of the abortive 1960 coup.

---

*Since this perjorative term has entered our war vocabulary, it is used throughout to identify the National Liberation Front's military arm.

A dedicated group of reporters filed stories from Vietnam, saying we were losing the war despite glowing official reports. One was David Halberstam of the *Times*, whose reporting was so candid that President Kennedy suggested to the paper's publisher he be brought home. He was not, and later won a Pulitzer Prize.

Suddenly the American public became aware of a place called Vietnam where our government was spending huge sums of money to stop Communism, and an increasing number of American "advisers" were losing their lives in combat. TV discussions were held. Questions were raised about the corruption and repressions of the Diem regime; about favoritism shown Catholics over Buddhists; about Diem's brother, Ngo Dinh Nhu, the power behind the scenes, and Mme. Nhu, who had promulgated a morality code that forbade dancing.

Then came the greatest scandal of all—in the summer of 1963, organized raids by government troops on Buddhist pagodas, and self-immolation by fire of Buddhist monks. Now the Diem regime was a serious embarrassment to Washington. The CIA, the Diem-controlled *Times* of Vietnam charged on Sept. 2, was plotting a coup to overthrow Diem. Two months later the generals' coup came off on Nov. 1. Diem's palace was invaded and he and his brother, who had fled, were captured and assassinated. That was the day Gen. Paul D. Harkins, then commander of our forces in Vietnam, was quoted by *The Stars and Stripes, Tokyo,* as happily saying, "Victory . . . is just months away and the reduction of American advisers can begin any time now."

Victory—and reform—were as far away then as today. Since Diem's fall, South Vietnam has been ruled by a succession of six shaky governments dominated by the military, with brief interludes of civilian control. In June, 1965, Nguyen Cao Ky, an Air Force vice-marshall, became Premier.

When John F. Kennedy became President in January, 1961, the American-financed Diem regime had no support from the people and the Vietcong had the upper hand in the countryside. Yet President Kennedy could see no alternative to continuing the Eisenhower commitment. Given the Berlin crisis and the resumption of nuclear testing, he "undoubtedly felt," Arthur M. Schlesinger, Jr. writes in *A Thousand Days*, that "an American retreat in Asia might upset the whole world balance." Yet he used "to mutter from time to time about our overcommitment in Asia."

In May he sent Vice-President Johnson on an inspection tour. On his return LBJ urged that we make "a major effort to support South Vietnam." But at this time Mr. Johnson advised against the use of American troops in combat, warning, Schlesinger writes, that this would revive anti-colonial emotions throughout Asia.

Johnson's recommendation that U.S. Military Assistance and Advisory forces in Vietnam be greatly strengthened, was seconded by General Maxwell Taylor on his return from a mission. Kennedy acted on their advice and by the end of 1961 we had 4,000 men in uniform in South Vietnam, as compared with 685 when he took office. The previous December Secretary of State Rusk had issued the Government's first White Paper, declaring South Vietnam to be threatened by "clear and present danger" of Communist conquest.

In sending so many more troops, President Kennedy appeared to go against his own skeptical intelligence, just as he had in the Bay of Pigs affair. "They want a force of American troops," he told Schlesinger. "They say it's necessary . . . to restore confidence and maintain morale. But it will be just like Berlin. . . . we will be told we have to send in more troops. It's like taking a drink. The effect wears off and you have to take another."

In the State Department, Undersecretary George Ball shared the President's skepticism. James Reston recalls that Ball presciently warned: "If you go up to 15,000, you will commit the prestige of the United States and you will have to commit 300,000 Americans to redeem it. Do you want to do that?" Secretaries Rusk and McNamara were ready to take the risk.

In handling the crisis in Laos, where the 1954 Geneva settlement had broken down, as it had in South Vietnam, President Kennedy played a more constructive role. With patient statesmanship he worked for the little country's independence and reunification, eventually agreed upon at a 1962 Geneva Conference on Laos. That Agreement, too, broke down. But it brought clear gains, Schlesinger believes. "The defenders of Laotian independence were no longer against the United States but against Communism. The result was to localize the crisis, stop an imminent Communist take-over, place the Pathet-Lao in the role of breakers of the peace, block the southward expansion of China and win the American position international support."*

Faced with the continuing crisis in South Vietnam, President Kennedy was persuaded by overblown reports of progress, that our heavy commitment was bearing fruit. Some of the glowing reports are said to have emanated from the CIA, which played its part in elevating Diem to power and subsequently convinced both Presidents Eisenhower and Kennedy that he was so strong and able a man the U.S. had best hang on to him.**

In his State of the Union message in January, 1963, President Kennedy declared, "The spearpoint of aggression has been blunted . . ." Yet two weeks earlier, 200 Vietcong, in their first stand-and-fight battle, had shot down five American helicopters and killed three Americans.

In September, after Diem's Government had been shaken by the Buddhist uprising, President Kennedy philosophically told his press conference: "In the final analysis it's their war—they're the ones who have to win it or lose it. We can help them, give them equipment. We can send our men out there as advisers, but they have to win it."

---

*See also pp. 91-92
**N. Y. *Times*, Series on the CIA., Apr. 25 '66

Schlesinger denies the report that the CIA in Saigon were in on the generals' plot which brought down Diem. President Kennedy, he writes, had ordered that we keep hands off, since he estimated that the pro- and anti-Diem forces were about equal. Yet Ambassador Henry Cabot Lodge, who had been sent out to replace Nolting, sheltered in our Embassy for three months the militant Buddhist leader, Thich Tri Quang, who played a major role in bringing down Diem.

The day the President heard that Diem and Nhu were dead, Schlesinger recalls, "he was somber and shaken. . . . No doubt he realized that Vietnam was his great failure in foreign policy and that he had never really given it his full attention. . . . he had always believed there was a point at which our intervention might turn Vietnamese nationalism against us and transform an Asian civil conflict into a white man's war. When he came into office, 2,000 American troops were in Vietnam. Now there were 16,000. How many more could there be before we passed the point?"

President Kennedy was himself assassinated three weeks later.)

VI
Johnson Says,
"This is War"

During his first year in office President Johnson stepped up our support of the shaky South Vietnamese juntas which rapidly succeeded each other after Diem's fall. By August, 1964, our forces there totalled 25,000. But they were to be used in combat "only as a last resort."

"I want to be very cautious and careful," the President said in a campaign speech on Sept. 28, "and use force only as a last resort when I start dropping bombs that are likely to involve American boys in war in Asia with 700 million Chinese. . . ."

The President's critics believe he had been neither "cautious" nor "careful" when in July of that year he rejected UN Secretary General U Thant's proposal, then backed by the U.S.S.R. and China as well as France, that the Geneva Conference be reconvened.

The public was shocked when it learned a year after the election, from Eric Sevareid's publication of his last interview with Adlai Stevenson, that Hanoi had offered in the fall of '64 to meet the U.S. in Burma for talks. Tardily admitting that the overture had been made, the State Department said Secretary Rusk had rejected it as "insincere."

Shortly after his overwhelming victory at the polls, President Johnson moved toward full-scale war. On February 7, 1965, we started round-the-clock bombing of North Vietnam. That was the day the USSR's Premier Kosygin was in Hanoi. He was presumably on a peace mission, since Peking was bitterly accusing Russia of trying to promote a settlement by calling for a new Geneva Conference. Russia had, in fact, approved President DeGaulle's proposal that the conference be reconvened, a proposal made at North Vietnam's urging, the *N.Y. Times'* Drew Middleton reported later.*

*N. Y. Times, Feb. 23, 25 '65

The Administration's response to DeGaulle was to say that we had given France no mandate to act as a mediator. When, at about the same time, U Thant suggested preliminary talks among the parties most directly involved, the White House, Max Frankel wrote in the *Times* of February 26, observed that there were no "authorized negotiations under way with Mr. Thant or any other government." The rebuff drove the Secretary General to declare publicly,

> the great American people, if only they knew the true facts and the background to the developments in South Vietnam, {would} agree with me that further bloodshed in Vietnam is unnecessary.*

It was at about this time that college teach-ins began and demonstrations against White House policy spread from coast to coast.

At Johns Hopkins, on April 7, the President lifted the hearts of his countrymen when he declared he did not find "power impressive at all;" called "the guns and the bombs, the rockets and the warships . . . all symbols of human failure," and offered to engage in "unconditional discussions." But peace discussions, analysis of the speech disclosed, would be held only with "governments concerned" {not, therefore, with the National Liberation Front}. At the same time, Mr. Johnson proposed a $1-billion regional aid program to develop the Mekong Valley for the benefit of the peoples of the two Vietnams, Laos, Cambodia and Thailand.

In mid-May, to mollify his critics, the President tried a five-day bombing pause, informing Hanoi through Moscow that there would be "a permanent end to the bombings if there were an end to Vietcong attacks in the South." Hanoi was scarcely given time to consult the South's National Liberation Front. But, as it later became known, Hanoi did on the fourth day send a message through France that she would negotiate on her own terms, without, however, demanding the prior complete withdrawal of U.S. forces. The message reached Washington a few hours after the end of the bombing pause.*

*N. Y. Times, Nov. 19 '65

27

On June 9, Mr. Johnson told his press conference that the open commitment of American ground troops to combat duty constituted no change in U.S. policy. Yet six months earlier, the Defense Department, in a question-and-answer pamphlet, had said the use of U.S. combat troops "would provide ammunition for Communist propaganda."

On July 28, the President said, "This is war." At his press conference on that day he announced the appointment of Supreme Court Justice Goldberg to succeed Adlai Stevenson at the UN, and for the first time explicitly supported free elections in South Vietnam "or throughout all Vietnam under international supervision." But he laid no ground for a truce. Instead he intensified air attacks on North Vietnam; increased our troops to 125,000 by September, and approved the construction of vast facilities.

"Jet airfields," the *Times'* Hanson Baldwin wrote from Saigon on November 28, 1965, "docks, ports, roads bridges, military quarters and even a city are being built by thousands of men and women and hundreds of earthmoving machines. . . . Never before in any war . . . has so much construction work been planned for one country in so short a time." Earlier, on August 27, James Reston had written from Saigon:

> The U.S. bases and supply areas are . . . on a scale far larger than is necessary to care for the present level of American forces . . . it is assumed . . . the . . . base at Canranh . . . is being developed into another Okinawa . . . as a major power complex from which American officials hope a wider alliance of Asian nations, with the help of the U.S. will eventually be able to contain the expansion of China.

"The word is being passed by highly credible sources," Robert Roth reported from Washington on September 26 to the *Philadelphia Bulletin*, "that we don't want negotiations now, that we would much prefer to wait until . . . our position is likely to be even stronger . . ." On October 20, the *Washington Post* disclosed that Secretary Rusk had said off the record that our policy was no longer one of negotiations but to achieve victory.

On November 20 a Hanoi peace-feeler was conveyed to the White House in a note from Italy's then Foreign Minister Fanfani, indicating that her only conditions for talks were a cease-fire and acceptance of the Geneva Agreements. The White House did not respond. On December 9, we bombed a large power plant in the Hanoi-Haiphong industrial complex.

As New Year's, 1966, approached, Americans dared hope for the gift of peace. The President had again ordered a pause in our bombing of North Vietnam. On the same day he started his whirlwind campaign, sending ambassadors to the world's capitals to testify to our desire for peace, but not, it has been reported, to offer any new basis for negotiations.

After 37 days, no signal having come from Hanoi, the President resumed bombing North Vietnam. On that same day, January 31, he formally asked the UN Security Council to arrange negotiations.

When the U.S. at long last turned to the UN, Sen. Morse observed during the February hearings, "it was with an olive branch in one hand and bombs in the other." As have other Administration critics, Sen. Morse charged that in taking armed action against the Vietcong and North Vietnam, the U.S. had violated the UN Charter, which provides, in Chapter I, Article II (4):

All members shall refrain in their international relations from the threat or use of force against the territorial integrity or political independence of any state or in any other manner inconsistent with the purposes of the United Nations.

And in Chapter VII, 39:

The Security Council shall determine the existence of any threat to the peace, breach of the peace, or act of aggression, and shall make recommendations or shall decide what measures shall be taken . . . to maintain or restore international peace and security.

Passing over this country's obligation under the Charter to have submitted to the Security Council our charge of aggression against North Vietnam, Secretary Rusk declared at the Senate hearings that we had acted in Vietnam under the SEATO Treaty, which, as we saw earlier, was signed in 1954 by Australia, France, Zealand, Pakistan, the Philippines, Thailand, the United Kingdom and the U.S., but not by such important Asian nations as Japan, Burma and India. By protocol the Treaty, as designed by Mr. Dulles, was extended to embrace South Vietnam, Laos and Cambodia, but the latter two countries said they did not want such protection.

The operative section of the SEATO Treaty, Article 4, provides that, if there is "aggression by . . . armed attack . . . against any of the parties or . . . any State or territory designated by protocol, each party will "act to meet the common danger in accordance with its constitutional processes" and such measures as are taken "will be immediately reported to the Security Council of the UN". The Article provides further that if "any party in the Treaty area . . . is threatened by any . . . situation {such as insurgency} which might endanger the peace of the area the parties shall consult immediately in order to agree on the measures which should be taken for the common defense."

Twelve years ago, when the Treaty was up for ratification—Arthur Krock recalled in his column of March 6, 1966, the Senate was given the following assurance by Sen. George, then Chairman of the Foreign Relations Committee: "{It} does not call for automatic action; it calls for consultation {with the other signatories}. If any course of action shall be agreed upon, then that action must have the approval of Congress. . . ."

When President Johnson started all-out war in Vietnam he did not consult Congress nor, as the leading SEATO power, notify the UN. Among the SEATO countries, troops have been contributed only by the Philippines—several thousand; New Zealand—one battalion, and Australia, which has recently raised its commitment from one battalion to a task force of 4,500. Moral support has come from Britain; disapproval from France.

"Our basic trouble in Vietnam," Mr. Krock commented, "is that we have not been proceeding under the Treaty but going it alone. . . ."

"It seems to me," Sen. Fulbright commented to Secretary Rusk, "this {lack of collective action by the SEATO powers} is explained by their not sharing your view. They feel it is a civil war . . . {not} an example of international Communist aggression. They don't believe their security is at stake."

Public knowledge that Mr. Rusk had brushed aside a number of overtures did not deter the President from extolling his Secretary of State, at the Freedom House function in February, as "a great servant of peace . . . {who} has sent the message . . . on every wire and by every hand to every continent."

VII
Aggression
or a Civil War?

"The evidence is overwhelming," Secretary Rusk told the Senate Foreign Relations Committee, "that the National Liberation Front is . . . intended to give support to the deliberate fiction that the war in Vietnam is an indigenous revolt. The Front is, as the facts make clear, an invention of the Communist Party of North Vietnam."

Disagreeing, Chairman Fulbright declared, "It is an oversimplification to say that this is a clear-cut case of aggression by North Vietnam, and not a civil war, as I believe it to be."

Mr. Fulbright is supported by Dr. Bernard B. Fall, who has devoted ten years of research to Southeast Asia and is one of the few non-Communist Western scholars who have visited North Vietnam. A French citizen who served in the underground against the Germans, Dr. Fall has lectured to U.S. Armed Forces schools, served as a consultant to government agencies, and is Professor of International Relations at Howard University.

In *The Two Vietnams* Dr. Fall demolishes the State Department's theory that "invasion from the North" is the *casus belli* in South Vietnam. "By mid-1963," he writes, "12,000 fighters may have come down from the North. . . . but that does not explain the extent or the persistence of the insurgency."

His view is shared by Philippe Devillers, author of the classic, *Histoire du Vietnam de 1940 a 1952*. "The initiative did not originate in Hanoi," M. Devillers wrote in *The China Quarterly* in 1962, "but {came} from the grassroots, where the people were literally driven by Diem to take up arms in self-defense." He points out that in the early years of the revolt in the South, Hanoi offered no help.

32

A third authority, Jean Lacouture, in his recent book, *Vietnam: Between Two Truces,* writes: "The war originated in the South and is being waged and suffered by the South, although with growing participation by the North." Recently a research fellow at Harvard, M. Lacouture is a long-time correspondent for *Le Monde,* has spent years in Indochina and the Mediterranean area and is an authority on "third world" problems.

In the March 3, 1966 issue of the *New York Review of Books,* M. Lacouture summarizes the events which led to the formation of the National Liberation Front. "Rural resistance to Diem," he writes, "spread further after the promulgation of the terrible law of 1959 which prescribed the death penalty for all 'accomplices of Communists' — and Communism comes cheap in South Vietnam." "At this time the resistance was composed of nothing more than Southern groups organized in self-defense against Diem. Hanoi had made no connection with them. The North Vietnamese did not begin to exploit this situation and infiltrate agents until 1959; and it was only after pressure from a Southern congress of 'former Vietminh resistants' in March of 1960 that they prepared to intervene. At the Northern Communist Party Congress in September of the same year, the Hanoi government gave direct encouragement to the revolutionary activities in the South. Still it was not until November 11, 1960, following an attempted military *putsch* against Diem, that the Vietcong, feeling the pressure of competition from military nationalists, gave itself a political headquarters by creating the National Liberation Front."

It appears ironically clear that Diem, the man this country sponsored and kept in power for nine years by contributing heavily to the support of his regime, triggered, through his sins of commission and omission, an uprising which has grown to such proportions that it has plunged the United States into a large-scale war.

The seeds of conflict had been under the surface ever since 1954, when the Geneva Conference split Vietnam in two, continuing the division made by the Allied occupation forces in 1945. But it was Diem who, with the United States' approval, refused to hold the reunification elections scheduled at Geneva for 1956.

The State Department has conceded that North Vietnam's armed attack began some years after the Vietcong went into action in the late 1950's. A legal brief presented on March 8, 1966 to the Senate Committee reads at one point: "There may be some question as to the exact date at which North Vietnam's aggression grew into an 'armed attack, but there can be no doubt that it had occurred before February, 1965."

The date selected marks the time when the U.S. began the bombing of North Vietnam and a substantial build-up of combat forces in South Vietnam.

In that same month the Department issued its second White Paper, declaring, "South Vietnam is fighting for its life against a brutal campaign of terror and armed attack inspired, directed, supplied and controlled by the Communist regime in Hanoi . . . many of the weapons and much of the ammunition and other supplies used by the Vietcong have been sent . . . from Hanoi . . . Communist China and other Communist countries have been the prime suppliers. . . ."

Yet the earlier, 1961 White Paper said the Vietcong's weapons were "largely French—or U.S.-made, or handmade on primitive forges in the jungles." Today North Vietnam is undoubtedly supplying weapons in quantity. But the Vietcong use, too, many American-made arms, captured in one battle after another. That they may also be acquiring quantities of new American weapons, Dr. Fall deduces from authenticated reports on the direct flow to the Vietcong of goods from American warehouses in South Vietnam.

"The evidence shows," the 1965 White Paper continues, "that the hard core of the Communist forces were trained in the North and ordered into the South by Hanoi." The fact is that after the Geneva accords, which called for a regrouping of armed forces, 80,000 or more Vietminh left the South for the North. There they may indeed have been trained, as Under-Secretary Ball charged in a recent speech, "in the arts of proselytizing, sabotage and subversion." It was doubtless these disciplined Communists, native Southerners, who started to filter across the demarcation line from 1960 on.

The 1965 White Paper states that "75% of the more than 7,000 Vietcong who entered the South in 1964 were natives of North Vietnam." Yet an examination of the personal data the paper gives on 23 infiltrees in 1964 shows that only six were born in North Vietnam. One diary found on a body read, "Leaving temporarily the beloved North to return to may native South to liberate my compatriots from the yoke of misery imposed by My-Diem {U.S. Diem} . . . I am proud and happy."

Figures released by our own military in Saigon on Feburary 19, 1966, show that of the total enemy force of 237,000, only 20,000 were North Vietnamese regimental regulars. The monthly infiltration rate, estimated at 1,500 in December, was reported to have reached 2,000-4,000. Even at this stepped-up rate, the troops from the North did not add up to "the tens of thousands" of armed men, who, President Johnson said at the Freedom House dinner, had invaded the South.

As compared with the South Vietnamese Government troops, the Vietcong have shown high morale and tenacity in fighting, with a desertion rate only one-tenth as high. In the spring of 1966, Secretary McNamara admitted to the Senate Committee, on May 11, that from 10,000-12,-000 soldiers were deserting every month, 85% of them conscriptees.

Under escalated American fire-power, desertions have also risen among the Vietcong. Defectors—the *N.Y. Herald Tribune's* Joseph Alsop reported from the field in March—say there is discontent in Vietcong-held villages over the heavy taxes now imposed and the conscription started in the spring of 1965. Previously the Vietcong had relied on volunteers.

Secretary Rusk has complained that at the time of partition "many Communists fighting with the Vietminh" were directed by Hanoi" to stay in the South, to hide their arms, and to undermine the South Vietnamese Government." The consensus among scholars is that upwards of 5,000 guerrillas in elite cadres did stay—either under orders or because their homes were there.

This small beginning can hardly explain the Vietcong's steady growth. In his new book, *Vietnam Witness,*

Dr. Fall points out that they added 173,000 to their ranks in 1965. "It has been stated," he observes, "that terror played a great role in recruiting that considerable force. How 64,000 men could force 173,000 to join them has never been explained . . ."

Correspondents agree that a good part of the country-side has been "liberated" by the Vietcong and that in many other "contested" areas they are strong by night if not by day. "What is Western-held in South Vietnam today," the *Christian Science Monitor's* Saigon correspondnet wrote in the spring of 1966, "is even by the most optimistic standards of Secretary McNamara, appallingly small in terms of terrain—though it contains 57% of the population." "The Saigon Government's writ," the *New York Times'* Neil Sheehan wrote, "largely covers only Saigon and other towns and major villages."

The National Liberation Front has infiltrated the cities and has an extensive underground in Saigon, where it has directed terroristic acts against American military personnel and adherents of the Saigon government. Writing in the March 12, 1966 *New Yorker*, Robert Shaplen reported:

> The Vietcong are still able to move freely through the metropolitan area, to control the waterways and many of the roads around the city, to reduce incoming supplies (and therefore increase inflation), and, in general, to keep their terror and propaganda activities going at a great rate. . . . there have been cases of Vietcong agents' getting up at public meetings or in theatres and making speeches. . . .

In its first broadcast over Liberation Radio/Saigon, in February, 1961, the N.L.F. announced it would "overthrow the camouflaged colonial regime of the American imperialists and the dictatorial power of Ngo Dinh Diem, servant of the Americans, and institute a government of national democratic union composed of representatives of all social classes, of all nationalities, of the various political parties." The new government would "improve the living conditions of the poor . . . reduce land rent, implement agrarian reform with the aim of providing land to the tillers . . . develop a national and democratic culture and education. . . . promote a foreign policy of peace and neutrality. . . ."

The president of the Front is a middle-class intellectual, Nguyen Huu Tho, a French-trained lawyer who stood high at the bar in Saigon until he broke with the French. In 1950 he led a student demonstration against the visit of three American warships and was imprisoned for the rest of the Indochinese War. On his release, in August, 1954, Tho formed A Commitee of Defense of Peace and the Geneva Agreements, to put pressure on Diem to carry out the accords.* Thrown into prison a few months later, he was rescued in 1961 by guerrillas and made head of the NLF. He was described in a Cambodian newspaper as one of those "authentic nationalists who had found it necessary to throw themselves into the arms of the Communists because of Diem's brutal policy." Queried about the characterization, Tho said he would not "object" to being so described.**

The NLF President impressed M. Lacouture as having "a grave, rather gentle look," resembling "the poet Boris Pasternak rather than a political leader, still less a military one." "In his interviews," this French observer recalls, "he was not very dogmatic. His thinking was colored by Marxism as was his vocabulary. But one did not receive the impression that he was a cog in a machine."

Two months after Diem had been assassinated and the Saigon Government was in the hands of General Minh's comparatively moderate junta, Nguyen Huu Tho, speaking as the Front's President, made an important announcement. If, he said, "the men . . . now at the head of the Army of the Republic will . . . break the chains of the foreigners in order to relieve their patriots from the evils of war. . . . the Front will do everything in its power to create conditions favorable to a solution of this kind."

This was an offer to Saigon to negotiate, M. Lacouture recalls, but "it received little attention since three weeks later General Minh was overthrown by General Kahn's more activist group. Thus the Front had to continue to battle. And it did, mercilessly."

"There were indications," he continues, "that Communists played only a partial role, even though they tried

*Fall, *Vietnam Witness*
**Lacouture, *Vietnam: Between Two Truces*

37

to infiltrate and control a wide array of different forces. Equally clear was the intention . . . of the NLF leaders not to appear as the executor of a policy dictated from the North. . . ."

M. Lacouture quotes a Canadian clergyman who observed in 1964, after living for several months among the Vietcong, that no more than 10% of NLF members appeared to be militant Communists. "Of course," M. Lacouture comments, "the 'common front' strategy that the Marxist-Leninists know how to conduct with such masterful skill does not require a large proportion of Communists to assure them of . . . power, provided circumstances are favorable to them. . . ."

Most analysts believe the Front's policies have from the first been controlled by leaders of the South Vietnames People's Revolutionary Party (Communist). Its secretary-general, Huyn Tan Phat, is not known to be a Communist but is believed to work closely with the Party. The Front's show-case Central Committee includes a French-trained physician; a Communist survivor of a French prison; a French army-trained tribesman who is also chairman of the Montagnard Autonomy Movement; a Catholic priest; a Cao-Dai leader, and a Buddhist Bonze, a member of the Cambodian minority, who joined the Front after his village had been shelled by Diem's forces.

The Front has reserved seats on its Central Committee for "representatives of political parties, mass organizations, the armed forces, and patriotic organizations" which may wish to join it. The vacancies have not yet been filled. For this reason, presumably, it has not so far tried to form a rival government. Yet the Front, in M. Devillers' view, has succeeded in consolidating "the most dynamic elements in South Vietnamese society."*

President Johnson sees the war in South Vietnam as a case of "insurgency mounted outside a nation." Yet all reports indicate that the Front is more solidly based in South Vietnam than the succession of non-elected, military regimes which could not have "survived for ten minutes," Dr. Fall has pointed out, "without U.S. military and financial aid."

*Viet-Report, Jan. '66

The Agreements reached at Geneva suited the Great Powers, save for the United States, but failed to ensure a peaceful future for Vietnam.

Arriving for advance talks on April 24, 1954, Secretary Dulles said he hoped "the aggressors would come to the conference in a mood to purge themselves of their aggression." To Mr. Dulles "the aggressors" were the Vietminh who, after fighting the French for eight years on their own native soil, had them under heavy siege. Foreseeing a settlement not to his liking, Mr. Dulles returned home and left Under Secretary Walter Bedell Smith to head the American delegation.

The Conference convened on May 8 — the day after the fall of Dienbienphu — with Anthony Eden and Vyacheslav Molotov as co-chairmen. The Asian countries represented were Communist China; Ho Chi Minh's victorious Democratic Republic of Vietnam; Emperor Bao Dai's recently constituted nationalist Government; and the kingdoms of Laos and Cambodia, where, respectively, the Pathet Lao and the Free Khmers had, in league with the Vietminh, been fighting the French.

Badly battered as the French were, they still held part of southern Vietnam, with the aid of Bao Dai's troops; but even in their stronghold, the Mekong Delta, they had been losing villages to the Vietminh. Ho Chi Minh was in so favorable a position that he intended to settle at Geneva for nothing less than control of all Vietnam, with sovereignty also accorded to the Pathet Lao, and the Free Khmers. Such a sweep would have been a signal victory for the Communists in Southeast Asia.

Ho Chi Minh had counted on the all-out support of Communist China and the USSR. But China had suffered heavy losses in Korea, feared American armed intervention, and Mao Tse-tung wanted to get on with economic development. The Russians were in a mood to trade Ho's soaring ambition for French defection from the proposed European Defense Community, which, if it had come into being, would have threatened them with a supra-national European army. Britain, for her part, was eager to further the *detente* with Russia to which Stalin's death in 1953 had opened the way.*

In the negotiations the U.S. delegation played a minor role, not wishing to be billed at home as approving a partial surrender to Asian Communism. Eisenhower recalls in his memoirs that at a Washington meeting in late June he and Churchill agreed that at least half of Vietnam must be denied the Communists. The loss of all Vietnam, Eisenhower reasoned, would threaten the position of other nations in South Asia, and eventuate in the "loss of valuable deposits of tin and prodigious supplies of rubber and rice."

The cease-fire which was signed on July 20, 1954 by France and Ho's Democratic Republic of Vietnam called, not for the surrender of the French forces, but for their withdrawal to territory south of the 17th parallel, and, conversely, for the regroupment of Ho Chi Minh's troops north of that line. Even though he held three-quarters of Vietnam, Ho settled temporarily for only half of the country, expecting to win all of it in the reunification elections scheduled for July, 1956. The Agreements stipulated that France was to keep civilian control of the South until that date. The cease-fire Agreements provided further for the unimpeded movement of civilians who wished to settle on the other side of the line; for no reprisals; for no increase in either side's armed forces, and for no military alliance with a foreign power. A separate set of Agreements stipulated that the Pathet Lao were to get no territory of their own but be integrated into the government of the Kingdom of Laos, and the Free Khmer accorded no rights at all in the Kingdom of Cambodia.

On the following day a "Final Declaration" was "noted," i.e., approved but not signed, by all of the Conference participants, save the United States and Bao Dai's Republic of Vietnam. This newly-created state, of which Diem had just been made premier, was represented at

*Donald Lancaster, *The Emancipation of French Indo-China*

Geneva by Dr. Trang Van Do. With no cards in his hand, Dr. Do had tried but failed to save Vietnam from partition and from what he foresaw would be complete domination by Ho Chi Minh once the scheduled elections were held.

At the end, all Dr. Do could do was to ask the Conference to "note" that, in spite of his "objections and reservations," his Government would undertake "to make and support every effort to re-establish a real and lasting peace in Vietnam" and would not "use force to resist the procedures for carrying the cease-fire into effect." Known for his high integrity, Dr. Do broke with Diem a few months later and was imprisoned. The promises he had made on behalf of his Government were not to be honored by Diem.

Presenting the United States' own declaration, Bedell Smith said his Government would "refrain from the threat or the use of force to disturb {the Agreements reached}, in accordance with Article 2 (Section 4) of the Charter of the United Nations, and . . . would view any renewal of the aggression in violation of the . . . Agreements with grave concern as seriously threatening international peace and security."

"The United States," Bedell Smith continued, "reiterates its traditional position that peoples are entitled to determine their own future and . . . will not join in an arrangement which would hinder this." He quoted a Washington statement of June 29, 1954 that called for UN supervision of elections "in the case of nations now divided against their will."

The fact was that the United States, France and Britain in planning the Vietnam negotiations, had deliberately bypassed the UN fearing that China's presence at a UN-sponsored conference would open the door to her admission.

Lacking any UN umbrella, the Agreements were to be implemented by an International Control and Supervision Commission on which India, Poland and Canada consented to serve. But the Commission's decisions in substantive matters had to be unanimous and it had no troops to enforce its rulings or to compel the regimes in the North and South to afford its inspection teams access to sites and individuals.

The Commission members arrived in Vietnam shortly after the accords took effect on July 22, 1954, and issued a press release. Citizens residing in one Zone would "be permitted and helped" to move to the other Zone if they so desired. No one was to be victimized. "Whatever you have done during the hostilities," the people were told, "will not be used by either side as a basis for reprisals or discrimination. A fresh page has been opened. Your democratic liberties have been guaranteed by both sides."

Unhappily, no "fresh page" was to be opened. Diem's police fired on a crowd assembled to cheer for peace in Quang Tri province, just south of the demarcation line. Eighty persons were killed and wounded, and the shooting continued off and on for three months.

The French High Command, the Commission said in its first Interim Report, issued in February, 1955, had failed to ensure effective civil administration in areas taken over from the Vietminh, with the result that "incidents resulting in injury to life and property have occured and continue to occur."

The Diem regime was to establish a pattern of violation of Article XIV, which not only prohibited "reprisals" and "discrimination" because of war activities, but guaranteed "democratic liberties." When the Agreements were drafted, it had not been foreseen that South Vietnam would be ruled by martial law rather than a civilian administration, as the accords assumed. The Commission was at a loss to deal effectively with a Saigon Government which repeatedly claimed "security reasons" for its violent suppression of all elements of opposition.

On the military side, the regroupment of forces by the French and Vietminh satisfied the Commission. Neither in this first Report nor in the five subsequent documents covering 1955 and 1956 is any mention made of the charge that North Vietnam early in the game violated the accords by increasing her regular army from seven to 20 divisions. But Dr. Fall notes that a letter of complaint was sent by Britain to Russia in April, 1956.*

*Christian Science Monitor, Mch. 14 '66

42

In its sixth Report, issued in 1957, the Commission noted that one of its inspection teams had been denied access to a military site in North Vietnam and had not been allowed to interview a group of {Catholic} seminarists as to their grievances. In South Vietnam, where, the Commission stressed, "the major part of its difficulties had arisen," its inspectors had not been allowed "to conduct reconnaissance and control of . . . airfields."

In its seventh Report, issued later in 1957, the Commission regretted that as yet no consultations had been held between North and South on reunification elections, and hoped the British and Russian co-chairmen would bring "to the attention of the Geneva Powers" the lack of progress toward a political solution.

In mid-1955 Diem had refused to hold the scheduled consultations on elections, saying he was not bound by the Agreements since they had been signed by a foreign military command—the French. He also refused to establish normal trade relations and in effect blockaded North Vietnam.

In July 1956, the month the elections were to have been held, Diem's police allowed a trained mob to wreck the Commission's Saigon offices.

Taking no responsibility for the fulfilment of the Agreements they had signed, the French pulled out of South Vietnam two months before the election date. They were content to let the United States take over.

Washington backed up Diem's refusal to hold elections. Yet President Eisenhower was to admit later in his memoirs, "Our direct interest in {the Geneva} negotiations arose out of the assumption that the United States would be expected to act as one of the guarantors of whatever agreement should be reached." Our spokesman at Geneva, Bedell Smith, in his closing speech took no exception to that paragraph in the Final Declaration which stated that "the military demarcation line" was "provisional" and "should not in any way be interpreted as constituting a political or territorial boundary." We could have fulfilled our duty as "a guarantor" and at the same time insisted that the reunification elections be UN-sponsored. Instead, we encouraged Diem to flout the accords by making the

17th Parallel a "political and territorial boundary," where he set up an economic blockade against the rice-poor North.

In a speech before the American Friends of Vietnam, Assistant Secretary of State Walter S. Robertson held the Agreements were void because North Vietnam had brought up guerrilla forces from the South and incorporated them in its military establishment. But this was the regroupment of forces for which the Agreements had called.

Agreements or no Agreements, Washington wanted no elections held because it knew Ho Chi Minh, who was regarded as the George Washington of Vietnam, would come out victorious. Later, in 1961, the State Department candidly said, in its first White Paper, "The refusal {to hold elections} came as a sharp disappointment to Hanoi. . . . {and} was a severe blow to the morale of the Vietcong in the South. . . ."

In 1957, the Commission reported "the introduction into South Vietnam of U.S. military personnel in five U.S. aircraft" along with "1,000 revolvers, and 610 cases of revolver ammunition." Diem's regime claimed the American personnel and supplies were "replacements" for units which had served the French, and held, too, that the U.S. Military Assistance Advisory Group had been increased only by transfers from the Temporary Equipment Recovery Mission.

In 1958, the Indian and Polish Commissioners insisted that Saigon furnish specific data on these transfers, while Canada held this was unnecessary. In another decision that year, India joined Canada in holding that South Vietnamese airports need not be controlled, Poland dissenting. From this time on, cold war tensions divided the Commission.

In 1960, India and Canada found not violative of the accords, Diem's infamous law of 1959, under which military tribunals imposed, with no right of appeal, the death sentence or hard labor for life for alleged acts of sabotage against the state. Their rationale was that the law did not specifically discriminate against persons who had been involved in the war against the French.

Diem now approved the Commission. But he could have been only partially pleased with its 1962 Special

Report, which faced two ways. Signed by India and Canada, this Report charged North Vietnam with "inciting, encouraging and supporting hostile actions . . . in the South." But it also charged that South Vietnam had violated the Accords by "receiving increased military aid from the United States" and that the setting up of a U.S. Military Assistance Command constituted "a military alliance."

The Polish Commissioner charged that his colleagues' Special Report was a weak indictment of South Vietnam, while it imputed to North Vietnam unsubstantiated violations.

It was to the Commission's 1962 Special Report that Secretary McNamara referred when he told the Senate Committee that North Vietnam's "aggression" had been "documented." He omitted to mention that in the same Report the Canadian and Indian commissioners had found a violation in the increased military aid Saigon was receiving from the U.S.,-aid which by mid-1966 was to add up to more than six times the number of troops sent south by North Vietnam, not to speak of our massive logistic support of the South Vietnamese Army.

From the start, Western observers agree, each side used or abused the Commission to serve its own ends. Both Saigon and Hanoi so balked the Commission as to make its efforts almost ludicrous. In 1963 and 1964 it submitted no reports.

On February 12, 1965, after the United States had started bombing North Vietnam, the Polish and Indian members issued a brief, tragic report. They quoted first the joint communique of February 7th in which the Saigon government and the U.S. Embassy announced that action was being taken "against military installations in North Vietnam" which "had been employed in the direction and support of those engaged in subversion in South Vietnam"; second, the telegram of February 8th from Hanoi protesting "the vile acts of the U.S. imperialists."

"These documents," the Polish and Indian commissioners declared, "point to the seriousness of the situation and indicate violations of the Geneva Agreements." They urgently requested the British and Russian co-chairmen to consider issuing "an immediate appeal to all concerned with a view to . . . preserving peace . . ."

In view of our Government's record, it seems curious that President Johnson should have told the American Bar Association in a campaign speech in August 1964 that "through the Eisenhower . . . the Kennedy . . . and this Administration . . . we have had one consistent aim—observing the 1954 Agreements." It seems curious, too, that for a full year after his re-election he resisted all proposals for a Geneva-type meeting.

Now, in 1966, the President sees the Agreements as "a reliable" means of guaranteeing "the independence and security of all . . . Southeast Asia." Secretary Rusk says, "All that is needed {to bring peace of Vietnam} is compliance with the Agreements of 1954."

History will judge whether the United States, which pledged at Geneva that it would "refrain from . . . the use of force to disturb" the Agreements, has not been the chief violator.

"In the provinces of Vietnam, the Communist Vietcong have been waging a revolution while the Governments of Vietnam and the United States have been primarily fighting a war," George K. Tanham writes in his new book, *War Without Guns: American Civilians in Rural Vietnam.* Mr. Tanham was associate director of provincial operations in Vietnam for the Agency for International Development in 1964, and is now Deputy to the Vice-President of the Air Force-sponsored Rand Corporation. Mr. Tanham's book was written in cooperation with W. Robert Warne, who was an A.I.D. provincial director in South Vietnam from 1962-64 and is currently with the State Department's Vietnam working group; Earl J. Young, who served in Vietnam from 1962-65 and is now Operations Officer of the A.I.D. desk in Washington; and William A. Nighswonger, who was with the A.I.D. in South Vietnam from 1962-64.

In his earlier book, *Communist Revolutionary Warfare,* a study of the Vietminh, Mr. Tanham wrote, "The crucial fact today is that the Communists are arousing the people to fight and work for them. It is easy but wrong to attribute their success solely to terrorist methods."

"The {South} Vietnamese need a cause and we have not supplied it," Brig. Gen. Edward Lansdale, Chief American Political Adviser to the Saigon Government, wrote in the October, 1964 issue of *Foreign Affairs.* As a colonel with the CIA, Gen. Lansdale was instrumental in Diem's rise to power. Today he points out that the 1947-52 American-Philippino struggle against the Huk guerrillas, in which he took part, was not put down until Ramon Magsaysay, a much-loved man of the people, became Defense Minister and made the constitution a living document for their protection. From then on the Huks lost support and had to go on the defensive.

No such leader as Magsaysay has appeared in South Vietnam and the Vietcong are still strong. The gains they have made, our Government insists, can be ascribed only to terrorism. But Washington appears not to credit its own propaganda. Ever since Diem's day, it has been urging one Saigon government after another to institute political and social reforms calculated to win from the Vietcong the people of the rural areas, who make up 80% of the population.

During the struggle against the French, the Vietminh turned over to the peasants, rent-free, land owned by absentee landlords and allowed the people to elect their own village councils. For a time, following partition, this pattern of life continued. After visiting some of their villages, Joseph Alsop, an inveterate critic of Communism, wrote in the August 31, 1954 *New York Herald Tribune:*

> In the area I visited the Communists have scored a whole series of political, organizational, military and one has to say it—moral triumphs. . . .
>
> The thing that impressed me most, in fact, was not the Communists' extraordinary feat of organizing, maintaining and expanding an independent state in southern Indochina without exterior support, and in the teeth of French power. What impressed me most, alas, was the moral fervor they had inspired among the non-Communist Viet Minh cadres and the stout support they had obtained from the peasantry.

When the Diem regime began its reign of terror, Vietminh guerrillas who had not gone north organized resistance groups among the peasants, and later went on the offensive. Now called by Saigon the Vietcong, they intimidated and drove out Diem's local chiefs, and assassinated the most odious. Looking back on these events, the Australian correspondent, Denis Warner, never a partisan of the Communists, wrote, "Summary Vietcong justice for a village chief guilty of corruption or brutality did not offend the peasants. On the contrary, it tended to endow the Vietcong with some of the characteristics of Robin Hood. . . ."*

*Denis Warner, *The Last Confucian*

Today the Vietcong are to be reckoned with almost everywhere. They are the masters of many "liberated" villages, where they collect taxes and food, recruit, run simple schools and clinics, and put on festivals that propagandize against "the American imperialists" and their "puppet" government in Saigon. In many other "contested" villages they hold the upper hand, by night if not by day.

The Vietcong have made headway, George A. Carver, Jr., explains in his 1965 *Foreign Affairs* article, "by concentrating on the peasantry and stressing the not entirely inexact theme that all Saigon governments have been urban-oriented instruments of the rich and the landed."

Formerly posted in the Saigon office of the A.I.D., Mr. Carver, it has recently been disclosed, is on the research staff of the CIA. He maintains that the Communist Party of North Vietnam is responsible for the insurgency in the South, and mentions only in passing "the shortcomings of the Diem regime." But he recognizes that the Vietcong have forged close links with the peasants.

"The average peasant's horizons," Mr. Carver writes, "are bounded by his villages, his rice fields, and the tombs of his ancestors. Wherever possible, the Communists have made this deep-rooted emotion work to their advantage by employing cadres and troops native to the areas in which they operate. This sentiment, by and large, has worked against Saigon regimes—particularly Diem's—which have usually assigned provincial administrators with regional backgrounds different from those of the peasants under their charge."

When the Vietcong employ terror, Mr. Tanham and his colleagues report, it "is usually but not always . . . on a selective basis, and designed to achieve a certain purpose. If there is a particularly unpopular and corrupt local offical, the Vietcong may decide to kill him in order to gain an image as the protector and defender of the people. . . . However no official, good or bad, is safe from Vietcong attack. If he is a good official, the Vietcong may threaten him several times and tell him to leave the area. If he does not do this (many do leave), they may kill him. . . . If there are several savage killings in

49

an area, government officials may quit. .... and essentially leave it to the Vietcong . . . Other terrorist actions have as an objective the intimidation of the people so that they will refuse to assist their own government and help the Vietcong instead. . . ."

The Vietcong, these four authors write, "are instructed to treat the people courteously and with respect, to pay for what they take, and to assist them whenever possible. They are also supposed to explain to the people why they are fighting and attempt to gain popular support. . . . Yet the Vietcong sometimes bring death and destruction. . . . In one instance they used the population of a village as a shield against the Vietnamese Army and forced the people to burn their own houses. . . ."

Relations between the guerrillas and the peasants appeared to the French jounalist, George Chaffard, to have been "harmonious for a long time," when he published in April 1965 a series on "Inside Vietcong Territory" in *L'Express*. But the early enthusiasm for liberators who had distributed land free, had faded to resigned acceptance, as the Vietcong found it necessary to impose taxes and conscript soldiers. In contested villages, taxes and conscription were being imposed by both sides. "The intensification of air raids and the . . . destructiveness of napalm and gas benumbed the rural inhabitants." M. Chaffard reported, "beyond any thought of revolt. . . . They want peace, any kind of peace. . . . the rural population is ready to swing to whoever is strongest."

The Vietcong fighters themselves have lost none of their ardour, M. Chaffard observed, noting that their regular units are mostly made up of relatives of Diem's victims. Their army is "incredibly egalitarian," with no insignia of rank among either the regulars or the guerrillas. "There are no salaries; a community assistance fund only provides some aid to families in the form of goods. . . . Some guerrillas who were already fighting in the jungles . . . before 1954, have never had enough time to marry, and, now in their forties, have never been with a woman. One begins to appreciate the amount of self-denial—of fanaticism—that these men have to have . . . to stick to the life of a resistance fighter."

That some Vietcong, under the stress of the war, may be falling from grace, is suggested by a captured document released by the U.S. military in Saigon. It was a political directive from the First Corps Vietcong headquarters, which declared that for their soldiers to have "carnal knowledge" of village girls was contrary to the philosophy of the People's Revolutionary Party.*

Mr. Tanham and his fellow writers point out that the Vietcong attract a following, especially among young people, even "while they kidnap youth, employ terror, and are harsh at times with the people." They picture the average youth as asking, "how can he get an education . . . a responsible and respected position . . . how can he share in the material benefits of modern life?" The youth is discouraged by "the local officials' corruption and the lack of interest," and the Government's failure to set before him "clear-cut goals that beckon him to serve {and} satisfy some of his, perhaps unconscious, ambitions and needs."

Under every Saigon regime, the social order has remained as stratified as it was under the French, who favored the educated and the urban classes. In the provinces today the great majority of parents cannot afford to let their children even finish grade school in the American-aided schools, Charles Burnham, an A.I.D. officer in Kinehoa Province, recently told the N.Y. Times' Charles Mohr. A high school diploma, he said, "can be obtained only by the children of the privileged classes which already control Vietnamese society and like it that way." Children of poor rural families are "permanently relegated to an inferior social position," Mr. Burnham said. "Primary education by itself," he pointed out, "only increases the frustration by encouraging the appetite. To these children the Vietcong offer the only real outlet for their energy."

In the same dispatch, Mr. Mohr reported that "Mr. Burnham and many of his colleagues in other South Vietnamese provinces tend to describe the continued preservation of privilege as madness."

Almost no Vietcong leaders defect, Mr. Mohr noted, "apparently because they know they cannot find any

*N. Y. Times, July 8, '66

meaningful, dignified place in South Vietnamese society. The Vietcong movement makes use of the native shrewdness and leadership capability of the peasant, but the Government will not because he has no degree."

In the view of "some American officials," Mr. Mohr continued, the social, economic and political aid which President Johnson promised at Honolulu is not enough. "An explosive social situation," one official told Mr. Mohr "is already quite obvious in South Vietnam. Few of {our} efforts upset in any way the established system. Increased employment . . . means first of all more jobs for those who are most skilled, and these are the groups, often urban, who are already on the Government side. Better agricultural techniques are helpful primarily to those who own land. . . . For the outcast, the rebel against the established society, a special program is needed. For him rules have to be changed, and until they are, he has no choice but to go on fighting for a change."*

*N. Y. Times, Mch 4, '66

X
Winning the "Minds and Heart" of the People

"The United States," President Johnson said when he gave Premier Ky his blessing at the February, 1966, Honolulu conference, "will give its full support to measures of social revolution, including land reform. . . . it will give special support to the work of the people . . . to build while they fight. . . . we will help them to stabilize the economy, to increase the production of food, to spread the light of education, to stamp out disease."

If the people of South Vietnam are still far from enjoying all of these benefits, it cannot be for lack of American dollars. The $675 million in economic—quite apart from military—aid which was disbursed to the Saigon Government in the fiscal year ending July 1 was double the sum provided the previous year, and was the largest amount disbursed to support a single country's economy in any one year since the U.S. began giving foreign aid in 1948.*

The rural reconstruction program, on which the A.I.D. has worked for some years, is not essentially new. Known in the past as "pacification," the program's primary aim has been "to win the minds and hearts" of the people and get the peasants on the Saigon Government's side. An expanded plan, drawn up by Gen. Lansdale, calls for the training in 13 short weeks of 59-man armed teams recruited from among the peasants themselves. The program has been directed and paid for by the CIA. But its control was transferred in mid-June to the Saigon regime when it was discovered that the training camp director, a CIA employee, was indoctrinating students with a nationalistic, but anti-Government ideology.**

By the end of June about 80 teams had begun to work in selected villages, while others were in training at the

*N. Y. Times, July 2 '66
**N. Y. Times, July 8 '66

Vungtua camp. Calling it "a promising development," the *Times'* Charles Mohr noted it was "a miniscule beginning in a nation of 15,000 villages."*

Borrowed from Communism, and reminiscent of Diem's methods, is the "population control" aspect of the Political Action Teams' duties. A census study of each hamlet is expected to unearth whatever relationships the peasants may have with the Vietcong. Every person must have an identity card. A trustworthy peasant, acting as the Government's agent, is to be responsible for units of four to eight families. Specially trained "Grievance and Aspiration" team members will interview each adult villager every ten days, ask what complaints they have, and try to have them satisfied.** But community grievances may be hard to deal with and remove, Mr. Mohr has pointed out, since "Vietnam experts generally agree that most peasants have been disaffected by arbitrary, unjust and corrupt practices of the administration and society."***

To help the people, team members will conduct rudimentary economic improvement and health programs, stimulate self-help projects, and encourage the election of loyal village councils, but if necessary run things themselves. Every inhabitant is to be inducted, again as in the Vietcong-held villages, into farmers', women's and youth clubs, all Government-dominated.

Newspaper correspondents have questioned the practicality of President Johnson's thesis that we can "build while we fight." They have pointed out, too, that this year's reconstruction blue-print covers only four areas comprising but 14% of the population.

The *N.Y. Herald Tribune's* Joseph Alsop detected "a big Madison Ave. element in all the talk about 'pacification' during the Hawaii meeting." He suggested that Washington was putting "the cart before the horse," since permanent pacification is impossible "before the villages to be taken in hand are beyond the reach of the enemy's regular regiments."

The theory is that after the armed Reconstruction team has in the course of three or four months indoc-

*N. Y. Times, June 29 '66
**N. Y. Times, Feb. 13 '66
***N. Y. Times, Feb. 13 '66

trinated the inhabitants and trained them in self-defense, and then left for another village, the villagers will be able and willing to keep the Vietcong out. This would appear unlikely in the Anlao Valley of Binhoa Province, where the Vietcong were driven out early in 1966 by our air-mobile troops. Visiting this area with Vice-President Humphrey, Tom Wicker of the *Times* reported the Vietcong had governed it so well for five years that they were popular with the peasants.*

As compared with the Vietcong, who have for years identified themselves with the peasants in their own localities, the Political Action teams, even if they are indigenous to the area, will be handicapped by their connection with the Saigon Government, always suspect to the peasants.

In Thuathien Province, the *Times'* R. W. Apple, Jr. reported on June 25, most of the P.A.T. cardres are ultra-conservatives. Some were used as political troops during the Buddhist crisis in Hue.

Describing some early gains made and the problems inherent in the Reconstruction program, the *New Yorker's* Robert Shaplen wrote in the March 12th issue, "No one (in South Vietnam) supposes that the Communist organization, so carefully built up over two decades . . . will be readily destroyed—if indeed, it ever can be."

It is Mr. Mohr's view that "the Vietcong still have a loyal, dedicated and highly disciplined underground political structure that operates in the heart of Saigon itself and in thousands of hamlets. So far the peasants have shown little inclination to inform on this structure or to help the Government actively. This is the central problem of the Vietnamese war."**

To "win the minds and hearts of the people," any Saigon government, whether military or civilian, would have to institute a genuine land reform program, which would be opposed by the urban and the propertied classes.

Of the most immediate urgency is the sky-rocketing inflation induced by huge U.S. expenditures, growing corruption, and a thriving black market. "U.S. Aid Keeps Making Vietnamese Rich Richer," the headline over a

*N. Y. Times, Feb. 14 '66
** N. Y. Times, Feb. 7 '66

January 1966 dispatch in the *Washington Star* read. In Saigon—the *Washington Daily News* reported on March 22—the Buddhist newspaper, *Fatherland,* protested that "the arrival of more than 200,000 foreign troops has upset the life of the population, bringing inflation and plunging the people into misery."

On June 16, the *Times'* Neil Sheehan wrote:
> While attention has been riveted on South Vietnam's political crisis, its economic crisis has begun to reach such alarming proportions that American officials here . . . fear . . . if inflation continues, it could cause even more serious political difficulties. . . . "The price of rice," one official said, "could put a lot bigger mobs in the streets than the monks could muster. . . ."

Observers doubted, a dispatch in the June 18th *Washington Post* read, that the Saigon Government's minor devaluation of the piastre "would substantially effect the country's galloping inflation."

The Ky regime has arrested and turned over to military tribunals hoarders, black marketeers and bribe-givers. But Government servants who solicit and-or accept bribes, and Americans who reportedly send tidy sums home, appear to have been immune from serious punishment.

In March a Chinese merchant was arrested, convicted, given 24 hours to appeal and was shot at dawn in Saigon's public square, while his weeping wife and eight children, pleading and fighting for a last word with him, were held off by the police. Sen. Young, D. of Ohio condemned "mock trials and firing squads." Another Democrat, Rep. Patsy Mink of Hawaii, denounced the "barbaric shooting," and said, "A thousand executed profiteers will not buy a stable economy or a new social order."

It might be recalled that Arthur N. Young, who was financial adviser to Chaing Kai Shek, wrote in his authoritative study, *China's Wartime Finance and Inflation 1937-45:* "The Government's inability to deal with the inflation, coming along with the disruption and suffering from enemy invasion, had a major part in making China ripe for revolution."

In the fury of the Vietnamese civil war, the peasants have been the pawns and the victims. Respect for human life and dignity have been tragically wanting.

Road mines, laid by the Vietcong, have killed peasants being transported in American buses to harvest rice in paddies near cleared villages from which they had been evacuated for protection from the Vietcong.

Early in April the UPI reported that the Vietcong had gunned down 25 chained captives when American-led South Vietnamese troops closed in on a jungle prison. The prisoners were mostly civilians and included three women. One of four who survived said the Vietcong had kidnapped himself and his wife because they had been friendly to Government troops. In another area, the *Herald Tribune's* Seymour Frieden reported in March, a Catholic priest was stabbed to death before the altar, five parishioners were killed and the church was desecrated. In an armed refugee camp, 87 refugees, some children among them, were killed. Of 1,559 civilians believed to have been killed by the Vietcong in the past year, Mr. Frieden said about one-third were school teachers.

Such dispatches give the impression that only the Vietcong are brutal. Testimony as to the cruelty of South Vietnamese soldiers, countenanced at times by American officers, comes from a former Master Sergeant, Donald Duncan, who served with the green-bereted U.S. Special Forces for a year and a half. Writing in the February, 1966 issue of *Ramparts*, Mr. Duncan recalls that when he reached Vietnam he was a highly motivated anti-Communist, having relatives who had suffered in Hungary. After carrying out missions behind the lines for the Special Forces, the be-medalled Mr. Duncan was so disillusioned he declined a captain's commission and was honorably discharged in September, 1965.

Mr. Duncan remembers "a couple of cases where it was suggested by Special Forces officers that Vietcong prisoners be killed." In a situation where there was not enough food for a unit of eight South Vietnamese soldiers and four prisoners whom they had inadvertently taken, a Special Forces major had hinted on the phone to Sergeant Duncan that the prisoners could be killed. Mr. Duncan was unwilling to take the hint, and the major later said, "You wouldn't have had to do it; all you had to do was give them over to the Vietnamese."

Further light on the Green Berets' operations has been shed by a University of Michigan anthropologist, Marshall Sahlins, whose visit to South Vietnam in the summer of 1965 was sponsored by the Inter-University Committee for Debate on Foreign Policy. In the An Phu district of the Mekong Delta, Dr. Sahlins was pleased to find a small Special Forces detachment who were giving medical and economic aid to the people—as though they were "the Peace Corps of the War Corps." But at another outpost he learned from an officer and a civilian aid that the Special Forces have "appropriated as their own, draconic Chinese methods of interrogation and indoctrination." Dr. Sahlins quotes Mr. X and Capt. Y as saying they try to teach their South Vietnamese trainees, when they are interrogating prisoners, to substitute mental for physical torture, not because the former is more humane but because it works better. The process involves converting the prisoner from Communism so that he will then give information voluntarily. "Torture is torture," Mr. X admitted, "and when you fuck around with a guy's mind and his whole basic *raison d'etre*, you're really hurting him." "If we do not break this guy," Capt. Y put it,"if we do not attempt to change his ideas . . . we've said that basically he's right." But most American officers, Capt. Y added, when confronted with the physical torture which the Government soldiers prefer, simply turn their backs "and go and have a cigarette."*

Villagers as well as Vietcong prisoners suffer at the hands of the South Vietnamese troops, Mr. Duncan reports. The former Master Sergeant describes how an air-

*Dissent, Jan.-Feb. '66

borne brigade, originally trained by the Green Berets, swept through a village. "They ...had the town in a grip of terror for three days . . . The Troops were accosting women on the streets . . . the police would just stand by." Rape, he reports, is a common offense among Government troops, but is severely punished by the Vietcong.

The troops, he continues, "would go into . . . a bar or cafe—and order varieties of food. When the checks came they wouldn't pay. . . . Instead they would wreck the place . . . American troops {were} told to stay off the streets at night to avoid coming to harm.

"The more often Government troops passed through an area the more surely it would become sympathetic to the Vietcong. The Vietcong might sleep in the houses, but the Government troops ransacked them. More often than not, the Vietcong helped plant and harvest the crops; but invariably Government troops . . . razed them . . .

"The people have suffered so much at the hands of the Government troops and now from American fire-power, that they prefer the Vietcong. The people remember that when they were fighting the French for their national independence it was the Americans who helped the French. It's the American anti-Communist bombs that kill their children . . . When . . . napalm burns their children it matters little that an anti-Communist Special Forces medic comes later to apply bandages. . . . One day I asked one of our Vietnamese helicopter pilots what he thought of the last bomb raid. 'I think maybe today we make many Vietcong,' he said."

The Vietnamese pilot's words, Mr. Duncan suggests, should be a warning to Americans who deplore the war and the bombings, but say they are necessary "to stop communism."

Mr. Duncan had to go to Vietnam to learn that "the world is not just good guys and bad guys." "Anti-Communism," he concludes, "is a lousy substitute for democracy." He doubts that Vietnam would be better off under Ho's brand. "But it's not for me or my government to decide. That decision is for the Vietnamese. I also know that we have allowed the creation of a military monster that will lie to our elected officials and that both will lie to the American people."

Not many Americans would consider Mr. Duncan's phrase, "military monster" accurate. But a good many would ask whether the men in the Pentagon and the officers who carry out their orders to napalm-bomb, shell, kill and injure helpless South Vietnamese peasants, destroying their homes and means of livelihood, have not adopted the Communist doctrine that the end justifies the means.

"The Saigon military communiques," the *N.Y. Times'* Neil Sheehan reported on February 15, "have failed to mention . . . the appalling destruction wrought in Giahuu and about 15 other peasant hamlets on the central coast, by artillery barrages and aerial bombardments." In three hamlets, about 1,000 peasant homes had been blasted apart or incinerated. In one village 100 persons were believed to have been killed and another 100 seriously wounded. At a field station Mr. Sheehan saw a woman holding a dying child whose legs had been horribly burned by napalm. Streaming along the coastal highway were some 5,000 homeless refugees. While the three-week offensive against four Vietcong regiments had killed about 1,000 guerrillas and Vietcong regulars, some American officials, "asked privately whether this might not in the end prove to be a pointless, if bloody, exercise." Pointless, because it was certain that when our troops left, the Vietcong would take over again. It seemed unlikely that the villagers' suffering and resentment would be assuaged either by the leaflets our planes were dropping explaining the Vietcong were responsible for the destruction since they had built their trenches and bunkers within the hamlets; or by Government brochures complete with photographs of Vietcong bomb atrocities in Saigon.

A local commander can burn down everything in his path, a veteran of many missions explained, "or he can spare those huts in the hamlet." "There are feelings of regret if women and children are among the dead. Some G.I.'s try to rationalize . . . by explaining that they {the women} were probably helping the V.C. or even shooting at *them*. . . . But no excuse is made when a child is found dead or wounded. . . . A conscience is not a good ally to have in this war."*

*Herbert Mitgang, *N. Y. Times Magazine,* May 22 '66

"I would rather do anything than make inspection tours of these burnt villages," an American officer told Jean Lacouture. As an adviser to the South Vietnamese infantry, this officer had to report to the U.S. Air Force on the bombings with napalm, which "burns the flesh and often hits women and children outside military targets." "Even," he added, "if it hits the Vietcong, the result is not very pleasant. . . ."

Saigon and Washington claim, M. Lacouture observes, that South Vietnam's unfortunate peasants are victims of Hanoi's *invasion* led by the Vietcong, and that the peasants are anxious to be delivered from the aggressors by nationalist and American troops. "But meantime waves of B-52's are bombing them, although the targets . . . are supposed to be military . . . can anyone who has witnessed the enormous destructiveness of {these} huge bombs doubt that this is a terror operation? . . .

An *AP* dispatch carried by *LeMonde* May 13, but not distributed in the U.S., read: ". . . the more heavily the Americans intervene . . . the more their reputation with the people decreases . . . in great part due to operations against the Vietcong in the course of which hundreds of villages are crushed. . . ."

Describing conditions in a provincial hospital, a *Le Monde* correspondent had in March found peasants of all ages, badly battered, two to a bed, sometimes three. "Abdominal wounds were numerous, inflicted by bullets, shell-bursts or bombs, grenades or mines." "Half-inflicted," the hospital doctor said, "by the Vietcong, half by the South Vietnamese or Americans." He estimated that "for every one who can reach a town, there are ten who died in the village or the fields or wherever they are struck." The reporter saw a boy of 12 in a wheel-chair, his legs "some sort of fearful reddish stumps, all that remained of his poor feet destroyed by napalm."*

That some American pilots have refused to fly saturation bombing missions against civilian targets is reported by the Swiss journalist, Fernand Gigon, in his new book, *Les Americans face au Vietcong*. A correspondent for the staid *Gazette de Lausanne*, M. Gigon tells of unnamed officers who have been relieved of their commands, reduced in rank and reassigned to the U.S., and of others who have resigned from the service in disgust.

Not to be forgotten is the story of Marine Col. Michael Yunck, who was hit by Vietcong fire in December 1965 while in a helicopter above a village, but decided not to order a napalm attack because of the women and children in the houses. As patriotic as he was humane, Col. Yunck, when he was having his leg amputated, invited in NBC's TV crew in the hope that "some of the draft-card burners" would see him on the operating table.

When, during the February hearings, Sen. Pell, D. of Rhode Island, asked how many civilians had been killed by our military operations, Secretary Rusk could give no figure. Later, on March 17, Repr. Zablocki, D. of Wisconsin, reported he had learned on a visit to Vietnam that "some recent 'search and destroy' operations had resulted in six civilian casualties to every Vietcong." He thought it "likely" that at least an average of two civilians were being killed for every Vietcong, which would have meant about 14,000 civilian deaths in January and February. But the Pentagon insisted that in seven months' time only 109 civilians had been killed, and 170 injured. The Pentagon figures were based on claims for civilian damages filed in Saigon. It would seem unlikely that most peasants who survived bombings would know they could claim damages for the loss of their families and their property—or hope to collect from Saigon.* *

A much-talked-of CBS film from Can Me shown on TV in early August, 1965, depicted U.S. Marines setting fire to thatched roofs with cigarette lighters and flame-throwers, as weeping women and children were led away. "The day's operation," Morley Safer narrated from the

*Robert Guillion, *Le Monde*, Mch. 12 '66
**Washington Star*, Aug. 19 '65

62

scene, "burned down 150 homes, wounded three women, killed one baby, wounded one Marine and netted four prisoners. These were old men who could not answer questions put to them in English and who had no idea what an identity card was. . . . If there were Vietcong in the hamlet, they were long gone. . . ."

Mr. Safer's news-cast caused him to be "checked into" by Asst. Secretary of Defense Sylvester, who was to tell former CBS News Director Fred Friendly that Safer "was very good" but "very tough on the military."

On January 6, 1966, the *Philadelphia Bulletin* reported that after a province chief in the Mekong Delta had declared all inhabitants south of the Vaico River were Vietcong sympathizers, our 173rd Airborne Brigade burned every house to the ground, smashed every cooking utensil, cut down every banana tree, slashed every mattress.

We use chemical sprays to destroy rice crops so effectively that we are now having to ship rice to a country noted for its fecund rice bowl; and we defoliate jungles, in every case warning villagers in advance by leaflets or air borne loud-speakers to quit the area, promising food and care.

The number of persons, mostly women and children, who had fled from their homes in the past two years had reached 1 million by early July. In May, Secretary McNamara told the Senate Committee 900,000 had fled from the Vietcong. A *Times* dispatch of July 5 reported that military operations by both sides have made many areas uninhabitable. Twelve thousand residents of Binhdinh Province, by American count, fled during "Operation Masher." A vast sweep involving a division of U.S. and South Vietnamese troops, the operation was later renamed "Whitewing." During ten days of fighting, a U.S. Army Civic Action team joined civilian officials in feeding, sheltering and giving medical care to the Binhdinh refugees. At the end of the fighting 9,000 returned to their villages, most of which are again under Vietcong control. The rest preferred to stay as refugees under the Government's wing.

As of the end of June, 1966, the Ky regime claimed that a third of all displaced persons had found new homes. But the *Christian Science Monitor* has reported that provincial officials frequently write off refugees as "resettled" when they still have no land or employment.*

The refugee camps, as described by the *Times*, range from sampans to primitive accommodations. Food and six cents a day is provided each refugee from U.S. funds, and voluntary agencies have their own welfare programs. The Monitor reported that provisions are often held up and that some province chiefs appropriate a fourth of the supplies for sale on the black market.

After visiting South Vietnam late in 1965, Sen. Edward Kennedy reported there were 100,000 orphans, and said he had visited a camp for 500 refugees where there was not a single toilet.**

President Johnson has declared "we have always hated the horrors of war;" has said he is carrying on this war "at the lowest possible cost in human life." And he has been quoted by the Secretary of Health, Education and Welfare, Mr. Gardner, as being "determined not to leave a war-torn country."

In a more realistic vein, the *N.Y. Times* has said editorially, "Of course, the United States has the manpower and the firepower to destroy the Vietcong—but only by destroying all of South Vietnam in the process. . . . No one wins such a 'victory.' Everybody loses. . . . The question is whether South Vietnam is to be treated as a friendly country, or, in effect, an enemy country to be bombed into submission with the consent of its unrepresentative national government, and then reconstructed. . . ."***

"It is my firm belief," Gen. Ridgeway has written, "that there is nothing in the present situation or in our code that requires us to bomb a small Asian nation 'back into the Stone Age'."****

Note at press time: In August, American military commanders were ordered to review procedures in order "to minimize casualties to civilians to the maximum extent possible." The order was issued after an American military spokesman had said casualties inflicted against civilians and allied military personnel since June had reached "epic proportions." (*N. Y. Times*, Aug. 17, 30 '66).

Christian Science Monitor, Feb. 5 '66
**Look*, Feb. 8 '66
***N. Y. Times*, Feb. 18, 20 '66
****Look*, Apr. 5 '66

On Memorial Day, 1966, when the President honored the several thousand American soldiers so far killed in Vietnam, his effigy had been burnt in the old imperial city of Hué; students had burned down the American library and consulate; troops of the South Vietnamese First Division were no longer taking orders from Saigon; the first Buddhist nun had immolated herself; and the leader of the Buddhist militants—Thich—Venerable—Tri Quang—was sending unanswered letters to President Johnson protesting Washington's continued support of Premier Ky.

Against this backdrop, the President declared in his Memorial Day Proclamation that the United States is "totally committed to the defeat of Communist aggression in South Vietnam." "We all know," he had told his fellow Democrats in Chicago on May 17, "that the road to peace is not the road of concession and retreat."

"Peace will come," Secretary Rusk told the Council on Foreign Relations on May 25, "when the other side becomes convinced it cannot achieve its purpose by force."

"We win," Secretary McNamara told the Senate Foreign Relations Committee on March 3, "if North Vietnam leaves South Vietnam alone."

The time to negotiate, Gen. Maxwell Taylor, the President's military adviser, told the Committee on February 17, is not "until it is quite clear their course of action is a losing one."

Yet the President has said there is "no single person anywhere in the world who wants peace" as much as he does. Mr. Rusk has said he is ready "to go to Geneva immediately whenever there is anybody there with whom to negotiate peace."

Despite the Administration's talk about readiness to negotiate, its policy of "ever-increasing force" has persuaded Sen. Fulbright that the President and his advisers really "want a military victory" and "unconditional surrender by the Vietcong."

General Taylor's testimony, the *N.Y. Times'* diplomatic correspondent, Max Frankel, wrote on February 18, 1966, "brought out in public . . . what other high officials have made increasingly plain in private—namely that the United States' terms for peace in Vietnam are much stiffer than the offer of 'unconditional' negotiations has implied."

Pressed as to our goals, Gen. Taylor said during the Senate hearings, that the U.S. "could, should and would achieve military and political successes of sufficient magnitude to force the Communists to accept an independent and non-Communist Vietnam." In the pursuit of this objective, Mr. Frankel noted, the Johnson administration "has never wavered."

In Sen. Fulbright's view, bluntly expressed to Gen. Taylor, the U.S. should be ready to deal with its principal adversary, the Vietcong, to seek "a compromise to stop the slaughter" and to give up a policy of waging a war that can end only "if all the Vietcong would go home and go north."

In his reply, Gen. Taylor said—as though he did not know the Vietcong forces, as distinct from the North Vietnamese troops, are indigenous to the South—that if they would stop trying to take over South Vietnam (and go North) they could at least obtain "compensation"—presumably through economic aid.

"Compromise," Mr. Frankel observed, "has had no appeal here because the Administration concluded long ago that the non-Communist forces of South Vietnam could not long survive in a Saigon coalition with Communists. It is for that reason . . . that Washington has steadfastly refused to deal with the Vietcong or to recognize them as an independent political force. It has offered to consider the Vietcong's 'views' . . . and even to let the Vietcong sit in the delegation of North Vietnam, whose agents it says they are. Washington's purpose at such negotiations would be to ratify the end of the Communist threat to South Vietnam and not to compromise on the basis of the existing military balance."

Sen. Robert Kennedy has pointed out that "a military victory at the cost of a 'completely destroyed South Vietnam would be a defeat for our larger purposes." In a ground-breaking speech in the Senate on February 19, he dared to suggest that the Vietcong be given "a share of political power and responsibility." "Whatever," he said, "the status of the National Liberation Front, puppet or partly independent—any negotiated settlement must accept the fact that there are discontented elements in South Vietnam, Communist and non-Communist, who desire to change the existing political and economic system of the country."

Sen. Kennedy specified there would have to be international guarantees, as "foreign forces {American and North Vietnamese}" were withdrawn "by balanced and varied stages."

With such a settlement, our responsibility would only have begun, in a sense. South Vietnam would need our help, Sen. Kennedy pointed out, "to repair the ravages of 20 years of war . . . to determine its own destiny and to live in harmony with the North. . . . Our reconstruction effort may be nearly as costly, and more demanding of care and intelligence, then is our present military effort."

Under Sen. Kennedy's "uniquely realistic proposal," Arthur Krock noted, the NLF would be represented in its own right at the negotiating table and allowed to participate in an interim government pending countrywide elections.*

"To include the Vietcong," Vice-President Humphrey objected, "would be like putting a fox in the chicken-coop. . . . an arsonist in a fire department."

From the viewpoint of a scholar who knows Vietnam well, Dr. Bernard Fall is convinced "it would be worth while, and for the most practical reasons of political-military expediency, to deal with the Vietcong as an existing *South* Vietnamese reality." "A more realistic appraisal of the Vietcong," he writes in an Epilogue to his latest book, *Vietnam Witness*, ". . . would finally permit the United States to regain a measure of . . . political initia-

*N. Y. Times, Feb. 27 '66

ive. . . . At the very least, it would increase the division between Hanoi and the NLF and would permit the emergence in Saigon of those elements which still command a measure of popularity and countrywide respect. Such elements still exist, but they can do little good if the penalty for even speaking of a compromise settlement . . . earns them an expulsion across the 17th Parallel—if not worse."

With Dr. Fall, the French journalist-historian, Jean Lacouture, fails to understand why the American Government, "which is struggling against the spread of Northern influence in the South" gives "the North the power to decide on war and peace below the 17th Parallel." "It is not up to the North Vietnamese," he holds, "to terminate a war in which they play an important but subordinate part. . . . Peace must be begun in the South, by Southerners, just as the war began there."

While Washington persists in discounting the Front as "a puppet" of Hanoi, officials confess their inability, Max Frankel wrote on January 1, "to judge the degree of Hanoi's influence over the Vietcong. . . . They do not know whether North Vietnam could negotiate an end to hostilities even if it wanted to."

Leaders of the Front are reported to be jealous of its independence, and not to have forgotten that at Geneva in 1954 Hanoi consented to a provisional partition of the country and forsook the South. In 1965 a high-ranking spokesman told *Le Monde's* Georges Chaffard that the Front had managed without the North for "a long time" and would prefer to settle our affairs among southerners. . . . We have not fought all these years simply to end up by installing one set of dictators in place of the old."*

Hanoi, for its part, in its four conditions for negotiations, has placed the greatest stress on the one which calls for "the settlement of the internal affairs of South Vietnam in accordance with the Front's program."

On paper—and from the few interviews that have been printed—the Front's political program appears more nationalist than Communist. When its Secretary General,

*Vietnam Reader, p. 260

Huynh Tan Phat, was interviewed by M. Chaffard in the spring of 1965, he said, "We will continue to fight as long as we have to, not to establish Communism, but to build a government that will fulfill the aspirations of the great majority of our countrymen, that is to say, a government which is neutral and democratic." To rebuild the country, the cooperation of the capitalist class and of foreign investors would be sought—"even U.S. aid will be welcome if she decides to respect our independence."

The Front's Secretary General said they would "not approach the problem of reunification for a very long time." He foresaw that "the economic and political structure which we will establish in South Vietnam . . . will differ more and more from that of the North." "To begin with," he explained, "we will gradually establish economic and cultural exchanges. When the time comes, negotiations for reunification will take place on a basis precluding annexation of one zone by the other."*

In theory, at least, President Johnson and the Premier of North Vietnam agree on autonomy for South Vietnam. "The affairs of South Vietnam," Pham Van Dong has said, "must be regulated by its own people." "The people of South Vietnam," the President has said, "must be left free to choose their own way, and no government, no regime, may be allowed to impose it by force."

In practice, for the past twelve years, Washington has supported a succession of Saigon regimes, from Diem to Ky, not chosen by the South Vietnamese people but acceptable to us because of their zeal for fighting the Vietcong. Advocates of peace have been executed, distinguished neutralists have remained in exile in Paris, and the South Vietnamese press is so strictly censored that columns of blank space frequently appear.

President Johnson has hopefully predicted that the elections which the militant Buddhists' April demonstrations forced upon Ky, will give South Vietnam "a constitutional government." But not within the immediately foreseeable future, it turns out.

*L'Express, Apr. 19 '65

The military junta, the *Times* reported on June 20, had thrown out the Electroal Commission's recommendation that the new constituent assembly of 117 members be given legislative powers. After it has spent six months writing a constitution, it is to be dissolved. This was one of "the minor modifications" in the electoral program to which President Johnson referred in passing in his Omaha speech of July 1. The election of a legislative assembly has been postponed until some time in 1967. The generals on the junta still appear to be making the decisions, even though ten civilians were added in May as a gesture to the Buddhists.

From Washington, on June 30, the *Christian Science Monitor's* Saville R. Davis reported, "A minority of the President's advisers" fear that "to intensify the drive for any elusive military success {as through the raids on the Hanoi and Haiphong oil tanks}" will "entrench the military dictatorship of Premier Ky . . . and frustrate the hope for a civilian government."

The consensus among Saigon correspondents has been that Washington and Ambassador Lodge will be well content to see Ky and his military junta remain in power until a military victory has been won.

"The governing junta," the *Times'* R. W. Apple, Jr. reported on June 25, "has embarked on a determined campaign to ensure that it will control, or at least dominate, the constituent assembly to be chosen in elections on Sept. 11." Phase One was promulgation of an election law that, "in the opinion of disinterested analysts, is weighted in favor of the generals." "Phase Two is quietly under way behind the scenes. It seeks a loose, temporary alliance that will help the junta to win election of assembly delegates friendly to it." In Hué, the Buddhist stronghold, the junta is attempting to foster a coalition between the Dai Viet nationalists and the Roman Catholics.

All candidates who have Communist or neutralist inclinations, the junta has decreed, will be ruled off the ballot. There are "no detailed safeguards," Mr. Apple notes, "for candidates who may be suppressed in this way." The elections are to be administered by district and province chiefs who owe their positions to Saigon.

They will decide who will be allowed to run, and which candidates will be given radio time, military protection and transportation, while on speaking tours.*

Saigon can hold elections only in secure areas, and in "contested" areas if the Vietcong do not interfere. Saigon claims to control about 50% of the population, mainly in the urban centers, while the Vietcong claim about 60% of the population and four-fifths of the land area.**

Presumably at Washington's urging, Premier Ky asked the UN to send a team to "witness" the elections—a request that had no chance before the Security Council since Russia could not countenance elections that would exclude the NLF. UN Ambassador Goldberg's subsequent suggestion that the Geneva Conference's International Control Commission be called in, would have value only if the Commission's Canadian, Indian and Polish members were given a mandate not just to "observe" a truncated election, but to draw up the rules for free elections and conduct them, with neutral troops at their command.

Even though the September 11 elections are to be run by the junta, they could conceivably bring some surprises to Ky, if the war weariness among diverse groups is as great as reported. But no predictions can be safely made. On the issue of negotiations vs. victory, the Unified Buddhist Church is itself divided.

Described as the best organized political force in South Vietnam, the Unified Church claims as members one million of the 13 million South Vietnamese who follow the faith in some form. The moderate Thich Tam Chau, head of the Secular Affairs Institute, has been willing to negotiate with Ky, while protesting his invasion of the pagodas. "Because I am a Buddhist," Chau has said, "I take a strongly anti-Communist position."***

Chau's rival for power, Thich Tri Quang, is generally described as a neutralist, although he has said his only interest is in getting a civilian government. In 1963 he gained a reputation for political power when he succeeded with the generals' help, in bringing down Diem. In 1966,

*Christian Science Monitor, June 29 '66
**N. Y. Times, Review of the Week, June 26 '66
***N. Y. Times, June 8 '66

neither the nuns' immolations, nor his own hunger strike, said to have worsened his asthmatic condition, proved effective weapons against Ky. By the end of June, Tri Quang had been taken into custody by Ky and moved from Hué to a Saigon hospital.

Tri Quang has said he "hates" the U.S. Government because it supports Ky. In its April 22nd cover-story, *Time* noted that while Tri Quang is "well aware of what he calls 'the destructive forces' in Communism and is openly contemptuous of the kept Buddhists in North Vietnam, he clearly feels that Communism may not be the worst enemy."

At Hué, in April, Tri Quang told a crowd of 5,000:

> We are oppressed by two pressures—the Communists and the Americans . . . We must regain the right of self-determination. Any nation when coming into another nation to help or rule it—through its aid—the first thing and last thing it will do is to annihilate the right of the local people to control their government.*

The Catholic support given Tri Quang in the Saigon Archdiocese in his drive for a civilian government in April and May was a sign of social and political change. In 1963, after he had overthrown Diem with the generals' help, tensions between the Catholics and the Buddhists rose to a fever pitch. Since the Catholics had been favored and protected by Diem, they feared persecution by the majority faith, and they feared, too, that the war against the Communists would slacken.

Today the Catholic leadership in Saigon, under Pope Paul's influence, takes a moderate position. In April, Catholics made no attempt to stop the Buddhists' street demonstrations in the capital. A liason office already established by Archbishop Nguyen Van Binh issued a communiqué which declared: "The most pressing problem . . . is the political vacuum. . . . The authorities are still unable to lay a legal foundation . . . and they still lack the support of the people."**

A January communique from the Chancery had read: "Peace can only be founded on a balance of military and

*N. Y. Times, Apr. 20 '66
**Joseph Kraft, N. Y. Review of Books, June 23 '66

72

political forces which would prevent the . . . destruction of either belligerent party" an indication that the Saigon hierarchy does not believe the war should be prolonged until the Vietcong are destroyed.

On May 24 a resolution was drawn up by "The Front of Civilians of Various Religions," and broadcast, inadvertently, one must assume, by the Saigon radio on May 26. The resolution was signed by three Catholics, including the popular leader, Father Hoang Quynh, who in the post-Diem period had organized a Catholic crusade against Communists; and by two representatives each, of the Cao-Dai and Hoa-Hao neo-Buddhist-military sects, the Protestants and a Buddhist group opposed to Tri Quang.

The resolution declared that after three years of military rule, the situation "has constantly and seriously deteriorated in all political, military and economic fields;" called for the resignations of Premier Ky and Chief of State Thieu, and for "a transitional civilian government," and exhorted the people and the Army "to unite . . . to realize the anti-Communist salvation struggle."

The next day the Buddhist daily which had published the resolution was shut for having printed "false reports."*

Probably an outgrowth of the first group, the formation of a Citizens' Religious Front was announced in Saigon on July 7, led by Father Quynh and Thich Phap Tri, a militant Buddhist. Other names mentioned were former Interior Minister Nguyen Hoa Hiep and Phan Ba Cam, the chairman of the Vietnamese Socialist Party. Their statement called for the immediate resignation of Premier Ky and transfer of power to civilians. It urged, too, a boycott of the Sept. 11 election.**

While in Saigon Roman Catholic officials cooperate with the militant Buddhists in working for a civilian government, strong anti-Buddhist sentiment persists among Catholics in the Saigon area who were refugees from the North, as well as among Catholics in the northern provinces. They are reported to fear that if the Buddhists were to gain political power they would not only move toward a negotiated peace but would attempt to set up a Buddhist state. On their side, the Buddhist leaders pro-

*N. Y. Times, May 27 '66
**N. Y. Times, June 8 '66

73

test they want a South Vietnam in which all religions can work together harmoniously.

Individual Catholics have taken a strong anti-war position. In a testimonial published in the February 2nd issue of *Informations Catholiques Internationales,* eleven courageous priests, noting Pope Paul's urgent appeals, declared the war had reached "a paroxysm of cruelty;" that "the presence of foreign soldiers" had brought "moral conditions which are an affront to human dignity;" that they could not "tolerate this absurd drama of brothers of the same country . . . attacking and killing each other in hatred." They called upon both sides to "renounce their ambitions of implanting or suppressing ideologies through subversion and bombardment," and warned that continuation of the war could "only lead to genocide."*

Another priest who had dared to cry out was quoted by Jean Larféguy in the October 2, 1965 *Paris Match.* "Today" — this country priest said of his parish, "Nothing remains . . .

> As for the poor mountain people whose villages and rice granaries have been destroyed, they can live only as wild boars in the forest. Before the bombardment, the loudspeakers, in the planes above them, told them . . . to stay in their huts . . . and the huts were bombarded anyway. Or again the Vietcong obliged them to come out and machine-gunned them in the fields. . . . I have seen my faithful burned up in napalm. I have seen the bodies of women and children blown to bits. . . . By God, it's not possible. . . .

"Suddenly," M. Larteguy recalled, "the priest burst into tears. His nerves had given way. He cursed the war and its attendant horrors and stupidities. He railed at the Americans in English, as if they were there to hear him."

Among intellectuals and civil servants—the NLF claims to have supporters in every government bureau—the strength of anti-war sentiment can only be guessed at. When Prof. Robert S. Browne, of Fairleigh Dickinson University, formerly on the staff of the A.I.D., revisited South Vietnam

*Commonweal, Apr. 1 '66

in the summer of 1965, he talked in Saigon with "a non-Communist intellectual" who bitterly recalled "the more than ten years of corrupt and inept government by the bourgeois classes which had succeeded in bringing his country only sorrow and destruction." Stressing he had no role to play if the NLF came to power—and indeed might be executed—Dr. Browne's friend declared he couldn't no longer deny them an opportunity to try their hand at government. He felt they were "the only Vietnamese who genuinely put their country's independence and dignity ahead of personal fortune-seeking."*

Dr. Fall suggests in his latest book that there are "large segments of the South Vietnamese population" that "have a certain stake in a non-Communist state . . . that would, in contrast with its predecessors, maintain viable relations with its Northern neighbor." He lists the Hoa-Hao and Cao-Dai neo-Buddhist sects; the Catholics; the *montagnards* (who are not ethnic Viets and dislike all lowland Vietnamese but will support any regime that grants them autonomy); the Catholics, and the nearly one million "Vietnamized" Chinese. These groups, Dr. Fall believes, could gain "a comfortable margin in any kind of a fair electoral test, provided {they} were not hell-bent on their own destruction—which . . . they have always been in the past."

What is really at stake in South Vietnam, UN Secretary General U Thant told the Amalgamated Clothing Workers on May 24, 1966, "unless an early end to the hostilities is brought about, is the independence, the identity and survival of the country itself. . . . There is growing evidence that the so-called 'fight for democracy' is no longer relevant to the realities of the situation. Twenty years of outside intervention and the presence of a succession of foreign armies have so profoundly affected Vietnamese political life that it seems illusory to represent it as a mere contest between Communism and liberal democracy."

South Vietnam's real permanent problem," Dr. Fall concludes, "and one that cannot and will not be solved by the presence of even a million American troops—is the

Viet-Report, Aug.-Sept. '65

reconstruction of the non-Communist body politic. . . .
Even a total military crushing of the Vietcong and the
wholesale destruction of North Vietnam are not very
likely to change the basic vulnerabilities of South Vietnamese society."

"With the bombing of targets on the outskirts of Hanoi and Haiphong," the *N.Y. Times'* James Reston wrote on July 1, 1966, "{the Johnson Administration} has now done almost everything it said or indicated it would not do except bomb China, and the end . . . is not yet. {It} said it was not seeking a military solution to the war, and it is now obviously seeking precisely that. It said it was {in Vietnam} merely to help a legitimate government defend itself, and it has ended up by supporting a military clique that is not a government, not legitimate and is not really defending itself . . . the guile of this Administration, exercised in the name of high and even noble principle, is hard to match. It was not going beyond the 17th Parallel . . . but went beyond. It was merely going to respond to enemy attacks on its bases, but it went over to the offensive. It was not going to get involved in a major war on the Asian land mass, but it did. . . ."

The Johnson Administration may, Mr. Reston wrote, "finally get over its agony in Vietnam—it may even achieve its military objective in the end—but it will probably never regain the confidence it has lost in its judgment and veracity."

The *St. Louis Post Dispatch* found it "a curious coincidence . . . that every American escalation of the war has appeared to come at a time when Hanoi was sending peace feelers, or international efforts for negotiations were afoot." "U Thant," the editorial continued, ". . . was reported last week to feel that there was some hope for peace talks if the United States would accept his recommendation for an indeterminate suspension of air attacks on North Vietnam. Instead, the air attacks were expanded and escalated. The new escalation may increase the cost of Hanoi's operations . . . but more importantly it will cost the United States untold sums of good will and esteem around the world."

"More than ever now," the *Detroit Free Press* said, "among the major nations of the world, the U.S. stands utterly alone. . . . Fresh questions are bound to form in the minds of much of the world about exactly who in Vietnam should be considered the aggressor."

The Washington Post, for its part, found "the practical military arguments for bombing the oil storage facilities of North Vietnam . . . compelling," but warned that "hope for the success of this attack must not be exaggerated" since the North Vietnamese have no great mechanized forces to be immobilized by a lack of petrol . . ." The paper added that "deliberate assaults on population centers" would be "overwhelmingly" opposed by "opinion in the United States and elsewhere."

The Washington Evening Star thought the President did not "owe an explanation to anyone," and the *Chicago Tribune* rejoiced over "this sudden infusion of courage into a vacillating policy."

The *Pittsburgh Post-Gazette* feared "this latest escalation will simply harden the Communist determination . . . and push the U.S. further and further toward an all-out war in Southeast Asia."

"It is a desperate day, indeed," the *Providence Journal* commented, "when the world's best hope for peace is that the Communist rulers of Russia and China will show greater restraint than has the President of the United States."

Administration spokesmen denied the bombing of the oil tanks was escalation. Secretary McNamara declared we were continuing our policy of "military restraint." Asked by the press whether any attempt had been made to warn the civilian population, he said "there was no special effort to do so," since the attack occurred in daylight and they had opportunity to be aware of it. The Secretary claimed "there were no civilians . . . in the area of the targets."

Agence France Presse reported that a mass evacuation of Hanoi had begun. The North Vietnamese Government was said to have ordered all residents in nonessential occupations to leave the capital, cancelling ration cards to force them to board trucks which began evacuating people the day after our first attacks on the fuel tanks.*

The raids on the fuel depots, Under Secretary of State Ball told the Foreign Relations Committee, probably involved fewer civilian casualties than the bombing of other targets in recent months. He estimated that the total of North Vietnamese civilian casulties so far was about 4,000 dead and 22,000 wounded—about equal to American military casualties in South Vietnam. We have done everything possible, he said, to limit civilian casualties and damage to North Vietnam's economy.

The attacks, Mr. Ball said, were "designed to speed the day when there can be a political settlement."

But Majority Leader Mansfield held "the destruction of petrol facilities won't deter infiltration." "It may slow it down for the time being, but the end result may be increased infiltration that will make the road to the negotiating table that much more difficult."

Sen. Robert Kennedy recalled that he and President Kennedy had several times made the mistake of accepting the assurances of top military men that the end of the was was in sight. "Had these calculations been correct," he said, "the bombings today would not have been necessary. Indeed, on each occasion the effort from the North has either increased . . . or taken a different and more dangerous course."

Sen. Aiken, Dean of Senate Republicans, his voice shaking with emotion, declared:

> The President is apparently taking the advice of the same people who assured him 18 months ago that a few days' bombing of North Vietnam would bring the enemy to its knees. . . . I think some of the people advising the President want to get China into the war one way or another. . . .

Sen. McGovern called attention "to the blunt fact that all but one of the South Vietnamese geneals who represent the military junta fought with the French against their own people." He condemned the latest bombing effort because it added "another dangerous new dimension" to the war, and "dodges once again the basic political issue of this conflict."

*N. Y. Times, July 3, 5 '66

The National Council of Churches sent the President a telegram that was not a direct condemnation of the new bombings, but said: "Increasing reliance upon military methods cannot produce a victory that can compensate for distrust and hatred because we are seen as a predominantly white nation using our overwhelming strength to kill more and more Asians."

It is true that the South Vietnamese generals have shown no scruples about having their fellow Asians in North Vietnam bombed. In a May 25th editorial the *N.Y. Times* charged that our initial bombing of North Vietnam can be traced back to a promise given in the summer of 1964, "presumably on Presidential authority," to General Kahn, who was then premier, as a *quid pro quo* for a pledge of governmental stability—which was never attained.

The President's former Special Assistant, Richard N. Goodwin, believes Mr. Johnson made the final, fateful decision early in February, 1965, when he "was advised that morale in South Vietnam could be revived only if we bombed military targets in North Vietnam." It was thought "this would assure Saigon of our determination to stay the course, and perhaps, if we were lucky, would so weaken Hanoi's will to fight that we could avoid the unpleasant, looming need to send in large numbers of combat troops."*

Our carrying the war to the North did raise the morale of the Saigon military, including Air Marshall Ky. A North Vietnamese by birth, Ky went on one of the first raids, and on landing said it had been "the most beautiful day" of his life—a remark faintly reminiscent of young Mussolini's delight in seeing his bombs burst "like flowers" over Spain.

The experts who had persuaded the President that bombing the North might "weaken Hanoi's will" and save us from having to send large numbers of combat troops, turned out to have had at best a murky crystal ball.

Today there are twice the number of North Vietnamese regiments in the South that there were eighteen months ago. By mid-June we had 270,000 troops on duty there—

*Richard N. Goodwin, *Triumph or Tragedy: Reflections on Vietnam.* First published in *The New Yorker*, Apr. 23 '66 ten times the number we had in Feb., 1965. By mid-June the U.S. Command in Saigon admitted to having lost 265 planes over North Vietnam and an undisclosed number of pilots.*

The count is mounting. On our second day of bombing the oil tanks, we lost four planes and three pilots, shot down by North Vietnamese anti-aircraft ground crews. Hanoi's defense capability against our bombers has been growing with the introduction of ground-to-air missiles launched from Russian-built sites, and Russian-built MIG jets, which in May started challenging our bombers in the air.

How a people who have known little but war for almost a quarter of a century have been mobilized for self-defense may be seen in the National Educational Television's film, "Western Eyewitness in North Vietnam," made in 1965 by the British reporter, James Cameron. One hears the American bombers zooming overhead, and the daily air raid warnings. One sees women with babies in their arms rushing to underground shelters. "The Americans," Mr. Cameron narrates, "have not yet sought to kill the innocent, but not all bombs fall on military targets. A tuberculosis clinic that was destroyed was in the line of a bridge."

The film shows men and women digging the trenches from which they will fire at our planes; shows them bringing in the crops with guns on their shoulders; pictures a woman militia leader displaying a wooden model of an American bomber, explainiing to her group, "This is what you must destroy;" shows a parade of peasants proudly carrying the metal fragments of a plane that had been shot down.

The American bombing, Mr. Cameron writes in his book, *This is Your Enemy,* parts of which appeared in the *N.Y. Times* in September, 1965, has provided Ho Chi Minh and his Government "with the most totally unchallengeable propaganda they could ever have dreamed of." "A nation of peasants and manual workers who might have felt restive or dissatisfied under the stress of totalitarian conditions had been obliged to forget all their differences in the common cause of resistance and self-defense.

*By July 27, 310 planes had been lost in the North.

From the moment the U.S. dropped its first bomb on the North of Vietnam, she welded the nation together unshakably . . . even in their own interests the U.S. planners failed to recognize the reality of a society like this: . . ."

·Hopefully, in March, our Air Force dropped over North Vietnam, along with napalm bombs, 3 million leaflets urging the people to give up the fight.

North Vietnam itself, Dr. Fall tells us in his latest book, has a half million men in its Class-One Reserves who have completed their two years of compulsory military training, as well as trained women specialists, who can be mobilized at a moment's notice. Dr. Fall has seen "reports and photos recently released from North Vietnam {which} show such units doing duty with anti-aircraft batteries shooting down U.S. planes over North Vietnam."

He reports, too, that the start of our bombing inspired "a countrywide propaganda campaign . . . termed the 'Three-Ready Drive' ('ready to fight, ready to join the army, ready to go wherever needed')" which is said to have netted a million and a half volunteers.

When truck convoys, bridges and roads are bombed, human labor, of which North Vietnam has a plentiful supply, is used for rebuilding, and for carrying supplies. In May, our giant B-52s' bombing of the key Mugia Pass was hailed in Washington as having crippled the enemy's supply system. But the pass was reopened in 24 hours.*

It is the view of the military analyst, Brig. Gen. S.L. A.M. Marshall, that our bombing of the North has been only .1 of 1% effective.**

"It is impossible," Gen. Matthew Ridgway has said, "to interdict the supply routes of an Asiatic army by air power alone. {In Korea} we had complete air mastery. . . . we clobbered Chinese supply columns unmercifully. . . . But we did not halt their offensive nor materially reduce its strength."***

Gen. Ridgway believes with Gen. James M. Gavin that we should, in our national interest, withdraw our

---

* *N. Y. Times,* May 14'66
** *The Mills of the Gods,* Canadian Broadcasting Corporation. Channel 13, N.Y.C. May 9 '66
*** *Look,* April 5 '66

forces to well-protected positions in the South and cease our war on the North.

Commenting on past errors of judgment, Gen. Gavin told the Senate Committee, "If I were a business man and looking at a potential market and found such miscalculation, I would have to do something about it. I would not long survive."

In 1962, Secretary McNamara said "the ratio of killed and captured" was much more favorable, "indicating that the South Vietnamese Army, equipped and advised by the U.S., was getting the better of the Vietcong. That year an American general told a civilian aide in Saigon, "We don't need psychological warfare. There are 20,000 Vietcong guerrillas in this country. We'll kill them and the war will be over." Reminded that the French had killed guerrillas for nine years but had lost the Indochinese War, the general said, "The French didn't kill enough. If you kill enough, you win the war."[*] He failed to see that a guerrilla war cannot be won without the peasants' support.

In May 1963, Mr. McNamara said, "The corner definitely has been turned toward victory." In October, just a month before Diem's fall, he and General Maxwell Taylor predicted "the major part of the U.S. military task can be completed by the end of 1965."

In February, 1965, after we had started bombing the North and the first contingent of U.S. Marines had landed at Danang, Mr. McNamara said they "probably" would not have to "tangle with the Vietcong."

In June, after the Marines were in the thick of it, Mr. McNamara assured an interviewer we were not moving toward "a land war" in Asia. In March, 1966, when American casualties were running more than 2,000 a month, the Secretary of Defense told the same interviewer we were not yet engaged in "an overt land war." It would only become one, he said, if substantial units of Chinese or North Vietnamese units were to enter the fighting under their own flags.[**]

[*] *N. Y. Times,* Review of the Week, May 15 '66

[**] Henry F. Graff, *N. Y. Times Magazine,* Mch. 20 '66

Estimating in May that North Vietnamese troops were infiltrating at the rate of at least 4,500 a month, Mr. McNamara told the Senate Committee they "are making war on the people and institutions of South Vietnam." He did not admit they might be moving south to combat a great military power which is bombing their country.

Mr. McNamara conceded that the April disturbances had reduced South Vietnamese military operations, but expected war operations would soon be back to normal. Five days later Ky struck at Danag.

In an article which heaps far more praise than blame on the Secretary of Defense, Stewart Alsop recently wrote: "The characteristics of the man—his filing-cabinet intelligence, his passion for being right, his profound distrust of emotion—fit him ideally for the infinitely complex task of 'rationalizing' a military force structure. . . . He has an absolute passion for collecting statistics about the war, and citing them to prove his points. But, as the intelligence expert warned him, 'facts and figures are useful, but you can't judge a war by them.'"

The intelligence expert, who was never called in again, had dared to continue, "You have to have an instinct, a feel. My instinct is that we're in for a much rougher time than your facts and figures indicate."*

The "kill ratio," reported each week to show a greater number of Vietcong killed than American and South Vietnamese soldiers, no doubt encourages Mr. McNamara. Yet he and the Pentagon have no statistics, as Secretary Rusk admitted at the hearings, on how many helpless villagers have been killed—and perhaps included in the "ratio." "There are," Dr. Fall writes, "hundreds of well-substantiated stories to the effect that this merciless bombing hurts thousands of innocent bystanders and that one of the reasons why few weapons are found in many cases is that the heaps of dead in the battle zone include many local villagers who didn't get away in time. . . ." As for dead Vietcong, correspondents report that the U.S. Command in Saigon sometimes announce up to five times

*Saturday Evening Post, May 21 '66

as many killed in a given engagement as have been definitely identified by officers on the scene.*

Mr. McNamara's computers must tell him that where there was one Vietcong fighter before, there are today two, their total force of regulars, local guerrillas, political and administrative cardres having increased between January, 1965 and May, 1966, from 103,000 to 207,000, exclusive of troops sent by Hanoi.**

His computers must show, too, that the vast country areas either held securely by the Vietcong or under their constant threat, have hardly been reduced, the South Vietnamese local forces having proved too weak to retain strongholds once they have been captured.

The military planners, a *Christian Science Monitor* reporter wrote on May 12 after a day at the Pentagon, admit that while "their forces have been dealing the Communists damaging blows in South Vietnam . . . the other half of their objective—seizing and holding population and land—has not materialized."

Twenty-five thousand air sorties are flown every week in Vietnam, Dr. Fall comments, "often with 200 planes in a single raid. And still, as they did 12 or 15 years ago, the little men keep coming, with their awkward, sauntering gait . . ."*** "Victor Charlie," the G.I.'s call the Vietcong.

What it comes down to is that with our jets and our napalm bombs; our secret "cluster bomb units" that contain 800 bomblets; our defoliation sprays; our helicopters which transport troops and artillery to otherwise impenetrable jungle fortresses; our radar for detecting the enemy presence; our ultra-sophisticated communications systems, and our machine guns that can fire 550 rounds a minute, we have so far been unable to defeat the Vietcong.

"As the casualty lists grow longer and effect more and more American homes," Sen. Fulbright told the American Newspaper Publishers Association late in April, "the {war} fever will rise and the patience of the American people will give way to mounting demands for an expanded war, for a lightning blow that will get it over with at a stroke.

*N. Y. Times, June 27 '66
**N. Y. Times, Review of the Week, May 15 '66
***N. Y. Times Magazine, Mch. 6 '66

The first demand might be a blockade of Haiphong; then, if that doesn't work, a bombing raid on Hanoi; and if that doesn't work, a strike against China; and then we will have a global war.

The day after the strikes at the oil tanks, the top military men in the Pentagon were reported to be looking forward to further escallation, aware that most of the steps they have urged on the President have, in time, been implemented.*

Gen. Taylor, the President's military adviser, wants to mine the harbor of Haiphong. Commenting during the Feburary, 1966 hearings, Sen. Morse said, "I cannot imagine Soviet freighters going through a mine field without the Soviet Navy first trying to get rid of the mines. . . . Putting mines anywhere around Haiphong is going to mean confrontations. . . . What would be American response to a mine laid by China or Russia in the Gulf of St. Lawrence?"

"Today," Mr. McNamara told the U.S. Chamber of Commerce on May 2, "it would be unwise and contrary to our interests to mine {the Haiphong Harbor}. The emphasis, the *Times* reported, was on the word "today," "for Mr. McNamara made clear he was not foreclosing such a step in the future."

In January, Mr. McNamara had admitted to the House Appropriations Committee, in testimony later released, that "we did not believe that so long as the Vietcong were militarily strong in the South, any amount of bombing—will cause North Vietnam to call off the aggression in the South."

The President alone, Mr. Goodwin assures us, "holds the vital decisions in his hands," but then notes that Mr. Johnson is "guided by the information he receives," and is "confined and influenced by his advisers."

The President's two closest advisers, Secretaries McNamara and Rusk, have in effect said this nation is not in control of its own destiny in Vietnam. Mr. McNamara told the Chamber of Commerce the number of American troops to be called up will be "in direct response to the step-up in the military activity by Hanoi and the Viet-

*N. Y. Times, June 30 '66

cong," and that we are "influenced by factors not entirely within our control."

"I would be misleading you," Mr. Rusk answered Sen. Pell in February, "if I told you that . . . I know where, when and how the matter will be resolved. . . . The nature of a struggle of this sort . . . is, of course, substantially determined by the other side."

Pressed by Sen. Fulbright as to whether China might not ultimately intervene, as she did in Korea, Secretary McNamara said on March 3 that the U.S. has disavowed any intention of destroying the Communist Government of North Vietnam or seizing its territory and that China has "no reason to fear military action by this country." But he admitted it would be "irresponsible" for him to say there was no risk of war with Communist China, in view of her "militant, aggressive actions against South Korea, India, and Nationalist China."

Secretary Rusk, in a March interview, conceded as to China that there is "a flash point" and said "both sides are being very careful," Knocking wood on his desk, he said, "We will be very careful."*

Correspondents found the State Department not overly careful late in April after an American bomber pilot flying near the Chinese border had reported he thought the pilot of an MIG attacking jet was Chinese. A Department spokesman told the press that Chinese pilots may expect to be followed over the border since we recognize "no sanctuary." The next day it was announced the President alone would decide if and when there was to be "hot pursuit."

Now that Communist China has exploded her third nuclear bomb, of a much higher yield than her first two, pressure may grow for a preventive war against her before she develops a delivery system, conceivably in two or three years. In Peking, Chou En-Lai said the U.S. had rejected China's proposal that the two countries make a formal pledge not to be the first to use nuclear weapons against the other, and that for this reason China had been obliged to develop her own nuclear arsenal. The State Department acknowledged that Peking had made such a proposal a year previously, and said the U.S. had rejected it as not representing "a constructive step toward the

*Graff, *Ibid*

paramount problem of controlled disarmament." But Department officials admitted, the *Times* reported on May 12, that the underlying reason for our rejection was "a reluctance to get the U.S. into a position {that} appears to foreclose on the use of a weapon that is viewed as a deterrent to Communist aggression."

Evidence that our military envisage the use of tactical nuclear weapons in the Vietnam War is to be found in Mr. McNamara's testimony before a closed session of the Senate Armed Services and Appropriations subcommittee, released in censored form late in Feb. 1966. Asked, on p. 107, by Sen. Margaret Chase Smith, "Under what conditions would you use tactical nuclear weapons in Vietnam?" Mr. McNamara said he "could not conceive of any in which we would use them in South Vietnam." Later, at p. 129, the Secretary's answer to a question from Sen. Mundt, part of which was stricken out, reads, "I said that we didn't at present conceive of any circumstances in which we would use nuclear weapons in South Vietnam. . . ." Whatever may have been said about the use of nuclear weapons in North Vietnam was censored.

In March, Mr. Rusk bleakly told an interviewer, "The American people are worried. They ought to be, because China is capable of grossly irrational decisions. . . . If we leave the impression with the other side that we can't face the risks, then we'll never settle these questions. . . . Most totalitarian countries make a mistake about what a democracy will do at the end of the day."*

Gen. Ridgway is convinced the risk of nuclear war is one we dare not take. "We have," he warns, "a potential for wholesale destruction so indescribably vast that many words, including 'victory', would lose their meaning.

> It would hardly be counted a victory if one football team were to defeat another through the use of knives; neither would we savor trimph in a 'victory' that would reduce three-fourths of the civilized world to rubble. . . .

"If our highest civilian authorities believe our goal should be {at whatever cost} the subjection of the world

*Graff, *ibid*

to American domination . . . then the American public should be told immediately. If our policy-makers do not believe in aiming for such a goal, and there is certainly no indication that they do, then a halt should be called soon to control our military build-up."*

Note at press time: When Secretary Rusk appeared before a subcommittee of the Senate's Armed Services Committee, normally a sympathetic forum for firm Administration talk about international security, widening doubts about U.S. relations with the rest of the world were expressed, the *N. Y. Times* reported on Aug. 31. The subcommittee was examining the implications of the military treaties which the U.S. has with more than 40 nations. Sen. Stennis, D., of Mississippi, declared, "The old lines are all gone, the old tests and safeguards, the caution we used to have, are all gone." He added that "the strained language of U.S. commitments could lead to new wars, such as that in Vietnam, with Congressional approval;" and that "about all that is left to us is to appropriate money." Sen. Stennis recalled that the only formal sanction sought by President Johnson for the Vietnam war was the Gulf of Tonkin resolution of Aug. '64, which he characterized as "pretty thin ice" to stand on. A second so-called Democratic hawk, Missouri's Sen. Symington, asked Secretary Rusk if the President could use U.S. armed forces to aid all of its 40 allies without consulting Congress. Mr. Rusk said he could not imagine this happening except in cases of "overwhelming onslaught." Sen. Symington noted that of 40 allies, only three—Australia, New Zealand and South Korea—have combat troops in South Vietnam. He predicted gloomily that should "some hidden tripwire" bring Chinese troops into the conflict, the U.S. would find itself in a world war virtually alone.

*Look, ibid

XIV
The Hope for Neutralization

Three U.S. Senators before long will visit Cambodia, a country with which we no longer have diplomatic relations. Chief of State Prince Norodom Sinahouk has asked that a delegation be sent to make an on-the-spot check of border areas where—our military have alleged—Vietcong and North Vietnamese troops have bases.

The senators will find Cambodia, in contrast with South Vietnam, unscarred by war, with no child beggars in the streets of Pnom Penh, its capital; a country whose five million inhabitants enjoy western-style democracy and freedom from foreign domination—the only one of the former Indochinese states where Communism has been "contained." The senators will learn, too, that Cambodia is progressing with a modernization program based on a mixed capitalist-socialist economy that is raising the people's standard of living.

In his book, *Cambodia's Foreign Policy*, Prof. Roger Smith of the University of Washington describes the Western nations, and from Communist nations; has trade astute Prince Sinahouk's policy of non-alignment vis-a-vis the great powers. Cambodia receives foreign aid from pacts with China, Japan, both Koreas, East and West Germany, and the Soviet Union; has close relations with France.

Towards China, Cambodia pursues a good-neighbor, but never subservient, policy. She has received foreign aid from China since 1956, and in 1960 signed a treaty of friendship and non-aggression with Peking. At the UN she has sponsored Communist China's admission to take the seat of Nationalist China.

In return, Peking has made no effort to dominate Cambodia and has damped down the Cambodian Communist Party. Six years ago she acquiesced in the deportation from Cambodia of a conspiring group of Chinese Communists. China may wish, Prof. Smith observes, "to impress Southeast Asia—especially those countries now allied with the Western powers—with the fruits to be gained from association with the Communist bloc. . . ."

Internal disruptions have been less of a problem in Cambodia than in South Vietnam and Laos, because the Prince is a popular and able leader. He stands high as a nationalist, having won independence from the French through skillful negotiations. He has introduced social reforms, and he out-maneuvered the local Communists by joining the neutralist camp at Bandung in return for promises of non-interference from China and North Vietnam.

At the start, Cambodia had confidence in the U.S., and was grateful for our economic and military aid. At Geneva, in 1954, the Pnom Penh delegation successfully held out for a provision permitting aid for self-defense — a concession also made to Laos. But Prince Sinahouk, Prof. Smith points out, did not allow Washington to meddle in its politics in the hope of changing its neutralist position. In 1963 he requested that we terminate the aid program and withdraw U.S. personnel. Anti-Sihanouk propaganda had been broadcast by the Khmer-Serei movement, from South Vietnam and Thailand, the Cambodians alleged, over powerful transmitters supplied by the CIA.

We began trying to shape events in Laos in the latters 1950's after the elections mandated by the Geneva Agreements and supervised by the International Control Commission had given the Pathet Lao, minority representation in a coalition cabinet headed by the neutralist, Prince Souvanna Phouma. Machinations by the CIA and the State Department, each promoting its own right-wing candidate, led to political chaos and to the growth in numbers of the Pathet Lao, successors to the Vietminh. North Vietnam connived with the Pathet Lao, and Russia sent arms, violating the Geneva Agreements, as the U.S. did too.

Reacting, President Kennedy threatened intervention by massing our troops near the Laotian border. But at the same time, showing more wisdom than he did in South Vietnam, he patiently worked for the convening of still

another Geneva Conference that would neutralize Laos.*
The Conference was finally held in 1962 and was attended
by 14 nations, including Russia, North Vietnam and
China. All agreed to the territorial integrity, unification
and neutralization of Laos. But before long, Hanoi violated
the new accords, and the Pathet Lao, withdrawing from
the second coalition government, seized territory. Today
the Pathet Lao, led by Souvanna Phouma's half-brother,
Prince Souphanouvong, controls that part of Laos through
which the Ho Chi Minh trail runs.

Like Vietnam, Laos remains a divided country and
is being sucked into the Vietnamese War. Blaming Washington for the Pathet Lao's gains over the years, Souvanna
Phouma said in a recent speech in Tokyo that in 1957
his coalition government was "greeted with understanding
everywhere except in Washington." He recalled that Secretary Dulles had taken the position, "If you are not
with us, you are against us."**

Yet Souvanna Phouma has had to retreat from his
neutralist position. He allows the U.S. to bomb Laotian
territory held by the Pathet Lao along the Ho Chi Minh
trail on which North Vietnamese troops make their way
south.*** And he allows the CIA to work in secret in Laos.

On a June visit to Ventiane, the Laotian capital, the
N. Y. Times' Harrison Salisbury learned that a line called
"Air America" but generally known as the CIA's private
subsidiary, supplies the "so-called aid projects that spatter
the map of Laos like a bad case of chicken pox." The
line makes night drops and air landings at more than
150 "U.S. aid" projects that "seem to require radio transmitters, occasional bundles of guns and possibly bags of
gold."

This type of aid is said to develop "islands of 'friend-
lies'" or little groups of the local populace who can be
counted on to fight back against the Communists. They
are supposed to set up informer networks and keep an
eye on goings-on in the back country.

In the northwest frontier area, Mr. Salisbury continued, political feuds "pale before the real interest in

*Schlesigner
**AP, *Christian Science Monitor,* Apr. 14 '66
***N. Y. Times,* June 13 '66

this corner of the world—opium." "There are skeptics who feel that several recipients of the bounty of U.S. foreign aid and of the CIA may have a deeper interest in the opium business than in the Communist business."*

For Cambodia, Prince Sihanouk made a very different choice. He finally broke relations in 1965 with the U.S. because Washington would not sponsor the international conference Cambodia wanted to guarantee her borders— a proposal North Vietnam and China were ready to accept.

Squeezed like a tiny Poland between Thailand and South Vietnam, Cambodia lives under the threat of incursions from her two ancient enemies. Centuries ago the people of the once great 600-year-old Khmer Empire were pushed back in the east by the ethnic Viets as they moved southward; from the north and west, in 1483, they were conquered by the Thais, who decimated their capital, Angkor Wat, and carried off Cambodians as slaves. Until the French came in the 1860's, Cambodia was ruled jointly by Vietnam and Thailand—or Siam, as it was then called.

To Cambodians today, the South Vietnamese, and the Thais, who have six times their population and could again gobble up their country, seem a much greater threat than China. Prince Sihanouk is said to believe neither of his neighbors would exert pressure on Cambodia's borders if the U.S. did not permit it.

As the Vietnamese war goes on, trouble multiples on Cambodia's eastern border. Our military have accused the Cambodians of helping the Vietcong, and Pnom Penh has accused the U.S. of a plot to drag Cambodia into the war. The Pentagon says our forces fire across the border only in self-defense. But a news dispatch from Saigon published June 3 disclosed that early in 1966 a battalion of U.S.-trained "Free Cambodia" troops, recruited presumably by the CIA among the ethnic Cambodians in South Vietnam, was secretly air-lifted to northeast Thailand to wage guerrilla warfare against Communist supply lines inside Cambodia.**

A few days after the publication of this dispatch, Thailand, in a counter-move that was conceivably in-

*N. Y. Times, June 13 '66
*CDN, N. Y. Post, June 3 '66

spired by Washington, asked the UN to send a team to watch over her border with Cambodia.*

So far as the South Vietnamese border is concerned, Cambodian officials concede—Harrison Salisbury reported on his Pnom Penh stop—that small units of the Vietcong can slip across the jungle frontier in many places despite the vigilance of their border guards. Cambodia's army numbers only 30,000.**

Prince Sihanouk has admitted supplying dried fish, rice and medicine to the Vietcong, but denies supplying either them or the North Vietnamese with arms and base camp areas.*** He has suggested that the Geneva Conference's I.C.C. team be expanded, at U.S. expense, in order to police the country's borders more effectively. Secretary Rusk has agreed to meet the cost. This will be a departure for Washington, the *Times* noted editorially on June 23. Not having adhered to the Geneva accords, we have never in the past contributed to the Commission's finances.

Prince Sihanouk has proposed that the expanded I.C.C. team:

(1) Investigate and control arms shipments into Sihanoukville, the capital's chief port.

(2) Check the movement of arms inside Cambodia.

(3) Watch the frontiers to prevent foreign incursions.

Because the Cambodian government has an over-riding fear of involvement in the Vietnamese conflict, it has opened up remote areas to inspection by foreign newsmen and diplomats. Mr. Salisbury reported that the senators are to be accompanied on their four- to five-day tour by Western military attaches.

The senators will discover in Prince Sinahouk a leader who, as I.F. Stone wrote after a visit to Cambodia early in May, has had "to make up for military weakness with political guile," a politician who, "in steering a skillful course between international rivalries and revolutionary pressures, has far outdistanced L.B.J. as a wheeler-dealer."

*N. Y. Times, June 10 '66
**N. Y. Times, June 7, 9, '66
***N. Y. Times, June 26 '66

At this point in time, Mr. Stone gathered, the Prince believes "the Vietcong will win and that his country's safety lies in cultivating good relations with the rebels and Hanoi."

The Prince's view of Americans, printed three years ago, is that they are "brilliant technicians and excellent soldiers," but "their incontestable realism stops short of the realm of politics, where the attitude of the ostrich seems to them to conform to their best interests."*

Sinahouk's foreign policy, as analysed by the *Christian Science Monitor's* Saigon correspondent, John Hughes, is "basically a sort of Peking-leaning neutralism" predicated on his estimate that "Communist China will eventually dominate the whole Southeast Asia area."**

As an advocate of neutralization, Prince Sihanouk convened the first Indochinese Conference at Pnom Penh in February, 1965. It was attended by delegates from North Vietnam, the Laotian Government, side by side with the Pathet Lao, the NLF and the South Vietnamese neutralists who have remained in exile in Paris—"bourgeois intellectuals" who were invited by the Prince over the objections of the Pathet Lao.

The upshot of the two-week conference was a resolution, drafted by the "bourgeois" gentlemen from Paris, proposing a Geneva conference on Laos and Cambodia that would inevitably lead to the Vietnamese question. An earlier resolution calling directly for a conference on Vietnam had been frowned on by the Hanoi delegation, which did not want to appear to have been pressured by the American bombing of the North which had just been started. The NLF delegates would have accepted the forthright resolution, Jean Lacouture reports. "No means to establish peace," they said, "should be excluded from the outset."

In a conversation with Prince Sinahouk, passed along by the latter to the press, the NLF Secretary-General, Huyn Tan Phat, said his delegation found "Cambodia a very contagious example" and wanted South Vietnam to have "the same way of life," to be neutral, and to receive

---

I. F. Stone's Weekly, May 30 '66
**Christian Science Monitor,* Mch. 4 '66

"unconditional aid from both the Socialist and Western camps."*

At the Prince's urging, the conference set up a permanent secretariat-general of the Organization of Indochinese People. But the beginning made at Phno Pehn, M. Lacouture comments, was ruined by American escalation of the war.

Cambodia has proved, Prof. Smith believes, that if the governments of the smaller Asian states can achieve modest social progress, pursue policies of reconciliation within their own borders and carry on normal relations with the Chinese, China will in her turn act as broker for their interests and not try to dominate them. In Cambodian-style neutrality, he concludes, lies the genuine third-way in the Far East,- independence and democracy as opposed to military or Communist dictatorship within U.S. or Chinese spheres of influence.

Neutralization of what was Indochina, comprising the two Vietnams, Laos and Cambodia, has for several years been a favorite theme of President DeGaulle. One must assume he believes it a sounder policy than the imperialist line he took when as France's Chief of State in 1945 he sent troops to put down the Vietminh rebellion against French rule in Vietnam.

The same prescription for peace in the area has been offered time and again by UN Secretary General U Thant, who has said that such a neutralization agreement would have to be guaranteed by the great powers, including the U.S. and Communist China. Recently Anthony Eden, who served as co-chairman at the 1954 Geneva Conference, has pointed to the desirability of a neutral belt of states south of China.

Sen. Fulbright has gone further. In a major floor speech on March 1, he proposed that "all of Southeast Asia" be neutralized. This would include Thailand, which the U.S. has made a strong bastion against Communism. There, the Senator said later in one of his Johns Hopkins lectures, "we are expanding our commitment in the same disorderly way {by which} we became so deeply involved in Vietnam."

*"Southeast Asia, A Special *Ramparts* Report," 1965

South Vietnam, Sen. Fulbright pointed out to his colleagues, "is only one of many small and weak nations on the periphery of a powerful China. . . . History and common sense suggest that a viable settlement in Vietnam must be part of a general settlement in Southeast Asia. Unless we are prepared to fight a general war . . . we have no alternative to seek a general accommodation. . . . As long as China and America are competitors for predominance in Southeast Asia there can be no lasting peace in that part of the world." Communist China, he suggested, might be willing to pay the price of such an agreement if she were confronted, as an alternative, with the prospect of permanent American bases on the Asian mainland.

Mr. Fulbright could have added that North Vietnam, the only other Communist state in the area, might be similarly motivated, that both China and Hanoi would benefit from open trade channels, and that Hanoi could reap benefits from the billion-dollar Mekong Valley development project which President Johnson has offered as a peace bonus.

Hanoi's openness to neutralization may have been reflected in a communique issued in Moscow on April 17, 1965. Dr. Fall notes in his recent book, *Vietnam Witness,* that a high-level North Vietnamese mission had gone to Moscow, presumably to nail down promises of Soviet support. "The joint statement issued following the . . . talks, contained little new in the way of precise Soviet assurances of military support, but it significantly reiterated the newly softened {Democratic Republic of Vietnam's} position on war aims . . . adding that the 'two parts of Vietnam {must} have no military bases and servicemen on their territory.' This seemed to mean that Hanoi conceded for the first time—at least in principle— that North Vietnam was 'neutralizable' and hence not an integral part of the Communist bloc, on a par, with, say, Hungary or North Korea . . .

these signs, considered in conjunction with the ingrained Vietnamese distaste for Chinese domination, the effect of United States military pressure, and the impact of the Soviet rift with China, suggest rather strongly that the present leadership in Hanoi might prefer to opt for a solution of the present situation which—in the words of two French commentators—would not make of 'the Vietnam war the Spanish {civil} war of the atomic age.'

Neither all or part of Southeast Asia could be neutralized, as U Thant and Sen. Fulbright have made clear, unless Communist China and the U.S., as well as other powers with interests in the area, were willing to guarantee the untouchability of the small nations concerned. Such guarantees, to be effective over the long term, should be under UN supervision. But China is not as yet a member of the UN.

Note at press time: As of late August, the plan for a Cambodian inspection tour by three U.S. senators appeared to be in abeyance. The visit to Pnom Pehn of Ambassador-at-Large Averill Harriman, which was to have followed President De Gaulle's three-day state visit, had been postponed at Prince Sinahouk's request, after U.S. planes, hunting for Vietcong infiltrators, bombed two Cambodian villages near the border on Aug. 2. . . . The ICC's inspection team had not been enlarged, the *N. Y. Times* reported on Aug. 31, because of opposition from Peking. Unable to settle border disputes with the Saigon regime, the Cambodian government had been negotiating with a delegation of the National Liberation Front, but there was as yet no agreement on the status of the Cambodian minority of half a million living in South Vietnam and that of the 300,000 Vietnamese in Cambodia. If the minority question is settled, the *Times'* Seymour Topping reported from Pnom Penh, Cambodia will recognize the NLF as the legitimate representative of the South Vietnamese people.

One of Asia's worst-kept secrets is Thailand's "audacious commitment" to the U.S. in the Vietnamese war, C.L. Sulzberger reported from Bangkok in the *N.Y. Times* of Apr. 15. "Forty-five per cent of all our bombing attacks against North Vietnam and many counterinsurgency and interdicting operations in Laos originate from bases made available to U.S. aircraft."

As a member of SEATO, which has its headquarters in Bangkok, Thailand signed in 1962 a joint agreement with the U.S., which pledged bilateral cooperation on the legal ground that "the treaty obligation is individual as well as collective." Under this pact the U.S. pledged to protect Thailand against either armed attack or "indirect aggression." "Thus, both militarily and diplomatically," Mr. Sulzberger noted, "an Asian second front has been created in Thailand."

About 25,000 U.S. servicemen, Peter Braestrup reported from Bangkok in the *Times* of July 1, are now stationed in Thailand, where our military build-up is "veiled in official silence." Two-thirds are air force personnel. The American-built bases from which they operate fly the Thai flag. An 11,500 foot runway at the new Sattihip base, on the Gulf of Siam, which can take B-52 bombers, was to be dedicated in August as the Royal Thai Navy Air Force Base—the Thai Navy having but one airplane. A dredge is deepening the harbor, and a 600-foot ammunition pier is being built along with storage bunkers.

To support our "second front" in Thailand, the U.S. has under way a $200-million military construction program which employs 7,000 Thais and 400 Americans. Two U.S. Army Engineer battalions are working on highway extensions for truck supply convoys. In northeastern Thailand, the construction of another major airfield at Khon-kaen was begun recently to accommodate more fighter-bombers.

A long-range plan calls for the creation of a logistics base for SEATO troops, "presumably mainly American," Mr. Baestrup writes, "who would come to Thailand's aid in case of Communist aggression." Enough arms, vehicles, and ammunition are already on hand to supply 17,000 American troops.

Calling itself "the Gateway to Southeast Asia," Thailand covers the largest area on the peninsula. With 30 million inhabitants, it is an uncrowded, currently prosperous country. Bounded by Cambodia on the east, it has a 1000-mile border with Laos to the north, and does not touch either of the Vietnams. Thailand is the only country in South Asia that kept its independence in colonial days—a feat which King Mongkut, of *Anna and the King of Siam* fame, achieved by playing off France and England, one against the other.

Thailand's king today is 39 year-old Bhumibol, who was born in Cambridge, Mass. and is best-known for his passion for the saxophone. But Bhumibol is in fact, Alex Campbell wrote in the March 26th *New Republic,* "a serious-minded king who . . . probably prevents the military {from} becoming too oppressive."

Since 1946 our military and economic aid to Thailand has totalled more than $1 billion. Our aid, Mr. Campbell estimates, made it possible for the last Thai strongman, the late Field Marshal Sarit Thanterat, who died in 1963, to amass a personal fortune of $150 million. Graft continues today, although on a less princely scale. "The Thai gross national product of about $3.4 billion is rising at about 6% a year and the ruling generals skim off much of the cream." To stay in power they depend on the 85,-000-man army.

Thailand has had no national elections since 1957. All political parties, save the so-called Revolutionary Party, were dissolved eight years ago. Members of the National Assembly are picked from the army, the police and the public services. This Assembly has been discussing for some years a constitution that would bring back democracy, and elections are supposed to be held next year.

In the universities there is criticism of the military regime headed by General Thanom Kittikachorn, but dominated by General Prapart Charusathien, who is Deputy Prime Minister and Commander-in-Chief of the Army. When asked about the U.S. bombers, General Prapart said they use the Thai bases "merely as fueling places."

"Two things," Mr. Campbell observes, "make the U.S. footing in Thailand slippery. One is that the people were never consulted . . . If these military men lost out in some internal struggle, the U.S. might find itself identified with a discredited military regime. . . . Americans in Bangkok are tempted to argue, and do, that the Thais aren't 'ready' for democracy. This verdict is inevitably tinged with self-interest."

General Parapart has flatly said, "There cannot be elections until every single Communist has been rounded up."

No infiltration of the cities has been reported so far. Some 800 guerrillas, believed to be inspired by Peking and Hanoi, are at work in the disadvantaged northeast provinces inhabited mostly by people of Laotian stock and by North Vietnamese who fled from French rule; and in the far south where there is a restive Asian minority.*

The Thailand Patriotic Front was formed a year and a half ago. From its clandestine Free Thai Radio, and from Peking and Hanoi, the peasants hear on their transistors that the Bangkok Government has "opened Thailand's gates to an invasion by the U.S. imperialists." To bark back and cover much of Asia, Thailand will soon have a giant radio station built with U.S. funds—the same facility which India declined, despite her quarrel with Communist China.

The American air-bases and build-up in Thailand, observers agree, give China and North Vietnam a powerful motive for driving the U.S. out of Thailand and upsetting the country's present regime. The *Times'* Seymour Topping has reported that Peking's threats led King Bhumibol, who usually stays aloof from politics, to tell his

*N. Y. Times, June 26 '66

people last December that a threat of Communist aggression, direct and indirect, faced the kingdom and that events might bring danger and hardship to Thailand at any time.* With her recent public commitment of small naval and air units to South Vietnam, Thailand has moved closer to the danger line.**

In the hope of forestalling Communist guerrilla activity in the impoverished northeast provinces, the Bangkok Government has started, with U.S. aid, a reconstruction program like the one laid out for South Vietnam. Mr. Baestrup reports that a 130-man U.S. Special Forces unit is providing training. "The neglect of decades," he writes, "cannot be overcome quickly." He adds that "the introduction of reforms has stirred new dissatisfactions by making the villagers more aware of the inequities of their status."

"Highly able economists and other civilians are trying to make Thailand a more decent country," Mr. Campbell writes, "but their advice isn't often taken and they can do little about the military graft. The military need them, but many of them are beginning to wonder if they, and Thailand, really need military masterminds like General Prapart."

Former Prime Minister Khuang Aphaiwongse, who was four times in office before political parties were abolished, and, in Mr. Campbell's judgment, ran one of the most uncorrupt postwar administrations Thailand ever has had, believes "the enduring answer to Communism in a country like Thailand is the sort of national unity that comes through wide participation in affairs by the people, in other words, political democracy."

But how, Mr. Campbell asks, "would the U.S. feel about elections in Thailand that resulted in a civilian Thai government with a somewhat more independent, less mechanically anti-Communist policy? Already the U.S. is toying with the idea of falling back on Thailand if things go worse in Vietnam."

*N. Y. Times Magazine, Feb. 20 '66
**N. Y. Times, July 7 '66

"The U.S. is getting a bad press, to understate the matter, throughout the world," a *Wall Street Journal* editorial read on May 24, 1966, when in the northern provinces of South Vietnam the civil war within a civil war was still to be crushed by Premier Ky. The situation emphasized, the editorial continued, "what has always seemed to us the heart of the problem: Is the U.S. getting hurt more than it is hurting Communism?"

To this writer, the heart of the problem lies deeper. Are we violating the moral law and American standards of decency by waging a war that cannot bring democracy to a people who have been long burdened by war, who have been given no choice and now see their country being gradually destroyed? Are we justified in sending American youth to die not to save, but to crush, a small nation?

When the President says that "liberals and intellectuals do not prize freedom for Asians as highly as freedom for Americans and Europeans," his critics answer that it is precisely because they look on the South Vietnamese peasants as human beings like themselves, that they want the napalm bombing and the bloodshed to stop. "There must be some moral limit," Gen. Ridgway has said, "to the means we use to achieve victory."

We are told that South Vietnam is the test, and that if we do not win there, "wars of national liberation" will be spawned everywhere. But we are reminded by Dr. Hans J. Morgenthau that every war of aggression is *sui generis*, that the Soviet success in Hungary and the Communization of Cuba have not to date set off wars of national liberation in other countries.*

New Republic, May 28 '66

Since the start of World War II, except for China itself and Vietnam—Professor of Government Donald S. Zagoria of Columbia University points out—the Communists have been unable to seize and keep control of a nationalist movement anywhere in Asia or Africa, so difficult have they found it to exploit nationalism to their advantage. In Indonesia, they surfaced for some years, and then fell.

The Communists, this Columbia scholar reasons, were able to take over all of mainland China; and the National Liberation Front, a good part of South Vietnam, by dint of capturing a war-created nationalist movement in the absence of effective opposition leadership.*

The President talks "as if Vietnam were one of the decisive battles of history," the *N.Y. Times'* James Reston wrote on July 3 after Mr. Johnson had spoken at Omaha. Calling his speech "a mishmash of bad history and dubious logic," Mr. Reston commented:

> It is hard to look ahead to the end of President Johnson's Administration and imagine this stable, free, cooperative world that will, in his view, be established by the sacrifices of Vietnam. . . .

> The President talked at Omaha about fighting for "the will of the people" in Vietnam but the will of the people there, so far as it can be determined, is for peace, while the will of the generals, whom the President is supporting, is for war.

"If President Johnson told us bluntly that we are in a power struggle to establish a decent order in Asia—which we are—and intended to establish American military bases at Cam Ranh Bay and elsewhere to maintain in Southeast Asia what he calls 'the vital security interests of the United States,' that, at least would be a policy. But he has not said that. . . ."

Secretary Rusk came close to saying it when he told the House Foreign Affairs Committee in August, 1965, that "the stakes in Vietnam" include "the rich natural resources" of Southeast Asia and "its great strategic importance." President Eisenhower made the same point when

N. Y. Times Magazine, May 1 '66

104

he wrote Churchill that the defeat of the French in Vietnam would undermine the United States' position in the Pacific.

If it is for the naked reason of maintaining our power in the Pacific area that we impose the horrors of war on the South Vietnamese, we should know whether by so doing we are diminishing or increasing China's power.

How, William Pfaff asked in the April 8th *Commonweal*, "do we punish China by killing Vietnamese?" "There is ideological intoxication in this, a treating of people and nations as though they were indistinguishable units in an ideological whole called Communism . . . There is also hypocrisy, and a kind . . . of cowardice."

China has no soldiers fighting in South Vietnam; no airmen flying for North Vietnam so far as is known; she has instead sent guns, trucks and other war equipment and an estimated 50,000 technicians, construction workers and railroad repairmen. By prolonging the war we serve China's interests; we sacrifice American lives and treasure, and we push North Vietnam and the National Liberation Front into an unwanted dependence on China.

"In the long run," Jean Lacouture observes, "the American war strategists will have done a good job for Peking. For if ever there was a solid, deep-rooted historical obstacle to Chinese expansionism, it was the Vietnamese nation. . . . Vietnam's history until recently has been nothing but a long resistance against China. . . . Should the U.S. decide not to help {South} Vietnam live under a regime of its own choice, should it elect to 'destroy in order not to lose,' should it continue to prefer dead Vietnamese to Red Vietnamese, China will have won a historic victory."*

It is said in Washington we will lose our world prestige if we stop short of victory. Actually, we are almost alone today among the larger nations. DeGaulle condemns our war in Vietnam; Prime Minister Wilson has qualified Britain's moral support since our bombing of the oil depots; Japan stands aside, and Prime Minister Indira Gandhi of India, the country whose delegate serves as Chairman of the International Control Commission,

Vietnam: Between Two Truces

has said the American bombing of North Vietnam must stop before another Geneva Conference can be called.

During the Committee hearings it was pointed out that Gen. DeGaulle gained—did not lose—prestige when he withdrew French forces from Algeria.

"Certainly," Dr. Morgenthau writes,

> this nation is great and successful enough for its prestige to survive the admission of a misadventure. But those who govern us do not seem to think so; for they are lacking in that measure of confidence in themselves, of inner strength, nay, of greatness which will give a government the courage to step before the nation and the world and say, we have been mistaken.

"It would be one of the greatest victories for us in our prestige," Sen. Fulbright declared during the hearings, "if we could be ingenious enough and magnanimous enough to bring about some sort of a settlement of this particular struggle."

The settlement, as Sen. Robert Kennedy has urged, would recognize the NLF as our principal enemy in the field and would provide for countrywide free elections in South Vietnam, the Front participating along with all other political groups. The elections and the implementation of the peace terms, including the withdrawal of both U.S. and North Vietnamese forces, would have to be supervised by an enlarged International Control Commission provided with troops from neutral nations, to the end that non-Communist and Communist South Vietnamese would learn to live together for peace.

It may well be that over the long term, South Vietnam's future as an independent nation will not be assured until both Vietnams, Laos, Cambodia and Thailand enter into a neutralization agreement guaranteed by the U.S., China and the other great powers. As Sen. Fulbright has said, "So long as China and America are competitors for predominance in Southeast Asia there can be no lasting peace in that part of the world."

Acceptance by Washington of such a pact would require a complete reversal of the policy we have followed in Southeast Asia ever since President Truman gave aid and comfort to the French, who claimed they were fighting not a colonial but an anti-Communist war in Vietnam. Would Washington be willing to give up our predilection for backing any dictatorial local regime as long as it is strongly anti-Communist, as we have for twelve years in South Vietnam, and eight in Thailand?

Commenting on the Senate's cutting back of the foreign aid bill and its refusal to authorize development loans to any country for more than one year, James Reston, on July 22, 1966 quoted Sen. Fulbright as having asked the Senate, "Is this foreign aid merely a tool and a part of a new policy of manifest destiny designed to establish our paternalistic control in Asia, or is it not?"

"There is a strong feeling in the Senate," Mr. Reston observed, "mainly as a result of Vietnam, that the President . . . is determined to maintain an American 'presence' in all the trouble-spots in the world, and is now talking more and more of an elaborate American policy of security for all of non-Communist Asia."

The Administration, it is true, has announced that it will give up our vast South Vietnamese bases once there is a return to the Geneva Agreements, and that it would welcome a neutral South Vietnam provided Saigon were left free to call on friends in case of danger. But Washington has said nothing about giving up its bastion in Thailand.

For the very reason that a neutralization agreement covering the small nations of Southeast Asia would put a period to both American and Chinese attempts to dominate them, Moscow might approve such an arrangement. But it would seem unlikely that Peking would cooperate so long as she is excluded from the world community.

In Formosa, on July 3, 1966, Secretary Rusk assured Chiang Kai Shek's Republic of China that the U.S. is "constant" in her alliance with her, and that "we oppose the seating of the Peiping regime in the U.N." He had no doubt this would be our position "for years to come."

A proposal that both Chinas be UN members and that the Security Council seat now held permanently by the Formosa Government be rotated among the larger underdeveloped states was made on July 20 by Sen. Edward Kennedy. Commenting at his press conference that day, President Johnson said the Administration is prepared to "do everything we can to increase our exchanges with Communist China," allowing businessmen, scientists and reporters to visit there; but he made it clear the U.S. will oppose her admission to the UN and continue our trade embargo until the Peking regime shows a willingness to abide by the UN Charter.

At the same press conference the President asserted we are not seeking a military solution to the Vietnamese conflict, and repeated that we are willing, "without any limitation whatever, to discuss any subject with the enemy {North Vietnam} at any time." Prospects for talks of any kind remain dim so long as we insist that Hanoi cease its aggression in the South and withdraw its troops; and so long as Ho Chi Minh insists, as he did again in his speech of July 17—in which he announced a partial calling up of reserves—that peace will not come until the U.S. ends "its war of aggression in Vietnam," and withdraws "all U.S. and satellite troops."

After American bombers had hit the oil storage depots on the outskirts of Hanoi and Haiphong, the Hanoi regime renewed its threat to try captured American war pilots as war criminals, hinting that they might be either executed or consigned to such strategic sites as oil depots and airfields.

North Vietnam, the *Times'* Foreign Affairs columnist, C. L. Sulzberger, wrote from Paris on July 20, may be using "the airmen as hostages to inhibit further U.S. moves to escalate the war." "When the first trial warnings were announced, Communist news agencies began to forecast American efforts to blow up the Red River dikes which control North Vietnam's main agricultural and population centers. Then, on July 14, the Hanoi Foreign Ministry accused U.S. planes of preparing to blockade Haiphong."

These would be the next crippling moves we would make, Mr. Sulzberger reasoned, "if Washington decides to tighten the vise further." "The Red River and its tributaries are now at their annual high level, and if the restraining wall is broken, floods would ravage the heart of the country. Likewise, were Haiphong isolated, North

Vietnam would be largely cut off from outside aid. The existing railway link with China is inadequate." "If logic prevails," Mr. Sulzberger concluded, "the prisoners should remain healthy until and unless there is a dramatic new American military move."

The President said at his news conference that the American public would regard the trial of American prisoners of war as "very revolting and repulsive" and would "react accordingly." He proposed a conference with North Vietnam under the auspices of the International Red Cross to assure proper treatment of all prisoners, but said Hanoi had rejected similar invitations extended privately.

Both the U.S. and North Vietnam—the latter in 1959—have pledged adherence to the Geneva Conventions which prohibit any and all "measures of reprisal" against war prisoners, including those who are tried for "acts committed prior to capture—" acts such as alleged war crimes or so-called crimes against humanity. But this latter provision was not accepted by North Vietnam and most other Communist states when they pledged adherence.*

That our partner in arms, South Vietnam, has made a practice of torturing prisoners, is common knowledge. On July 21, Ohio's Sen. Young told the Senate, the *AP* reported, that the South Vietnamese are executing many prisoners. The U.S., he said, "in the name of humanity should stop transferring Vietcong prisoners to South Vietnamese units." Three weeks previously our military had announced that henceforth Vietcong and North Vietnamese soldiers, when captured, were to be kept out of the hands of the South Vietnamese soldiers, and that the latter were to be "educated" not to use physical torture to extract information.** Whether the new policy has been fully implemented—or can be—is not known.

As distinct from physical torture, the U.S. Special Forces have refined technics of psychological torture, as an officer explained to Prof. Marshall Sahlins.*** While this method of eliciting intelligence is not specifically

* *N. Y. Times*, July 20 '66
** *N. Y. Times*, July 1 '66
***See pg. 58 above

prohibited, Article 3 of Geneva Convention III forbids "outrages upon personal dignity . . . in particular, humiliating and degrading treatment," and Article 13 rules out "intimidation" and "insults."

As the gulf between Hanoi and Washington was becoming apparently unbridgeable, the USSR turned down Prime Minister Wilson's urgent request that she join Great Britain in convening a new conference on Vietnam, the two countries having been co-chairmen of the 1954 Geneva Conference. Moscow had approved such a conference before we began bombing the North in February 1965; now she refused to move without Hanoi's approval.

In a formal letter to the Security Council circulated on June 30, the U.S. announced it had been forced to extend its bombing of North Vietnam because of "the increased intensity of {her} aggression;" and at the same time asked the Council to arrange peace talks either in a renewed Geneva Conference or "in some other forum." Ten days later the Soviet Union returned the letter, charging it was a "maneuver" to justify "expanding the shameful war" in Vietnam. Ambassador Goldberg accused Moscow of blocking negotiations.*

To the great disappointment of Sen. Morse and many other concerned Americans, the Security Council has made no attempt to bring about negotiations, as President Johnson first asked it to on January 31, 1966, the day he resumed the bombing of North Vietnam. There are two understandable reasons: Russia holds a veto, and of the countries directly concerned in the South Vietnamese conflict, only the U.S. is a UN member.

From Moscow, the *Times'* chief correspondent, Peter Grose, wrote in mid-July, "The question is no longer whether the Soviet Union wants to get involved in the Vietnam fighting. Clearly, it does not. The question now is whether the circumstances of the Communist world are going to force the Soviet Union into some kind of military action."** The Soviet Union and the other Warsaw Pact states had already announced they will send volunteers if requested.

---

*N. Y. Times, July 13 '66
**N. Y. Times, Review of the Week, July 17 '66, p. 1

Arthur M. Schlesinger, Jr., warns in an August 9th *Look* article that we are moving down a road that will rally the North Vietnamese behind their government, make negotiation impossible and eventually draw Communist China into the conflict. Increased Americanization of the war, he predicts, would make victory impossible because the war would become one of white men against Asians—an eventuality that President Kennedy himself foresaw.

"The more we Americanize the war—" President Kennedy's former aide writes, "increasing our military presence, by summoning Saigon leaders, like vassals, to conferences . . . by transforming the local war in Vietnam into a global test between America and China—the more we make the war unwinnable. . . ."

To end "one of the most barbarous wars in history," UN Secretary General U Thant, in his personal capacity, called again on June 20 for the three steps he believes to be essential prerequisites to a cease-fire: the cessation of the bombing of the North; the scaling down of military operations in the South, and willingness on all sides to enter into discussion with those who are "actually fighting."

Premier Ky is even less likely than Washington to consent to sit down with the NLF. So insistent is he on an all-out military victory that he evens talks of "occupying North Vietnam."* If there is ever to be peace, the U.S. will sooner or later have to "blow the whistle" on Ky, the *Times* pointed out in its May 25 editorial. Without our unstinted military and economic aid, he could not survive for ten minutes, Bernard Fall has reminded us.

Sen. McGovern declares he has "always found it difficult to understand the rationality of refusing to negotiate with the NLF." To quibble over the implications of recognizing the existence of the NLF when so many lives are being lost every day in warfare with them is nightmarish absurdity."**

Were the Administration to send peace-feelers to the NLF, no longer treating it as a puppet of Hanoi, a favor-

*Eric Sevareid, *CBS News*, July 5 '66
**N. Y. Review of Books, July 7 '66

able response could be less safely predicted than it could have been eighteen months ago. With every "Operation Masher," the will of the Front's leaders is reported to have hardened and their hatred and suspicion of the U.S. have risen to new heights, as has Hanoi's outrage over our bombing.

Even if Hanoi, failing effective intervention by China and/or Russia, is forced in time to admit defeat, surrender by the Vietcong would not necessarily follow. "The war in South Vietnam will continue," *The Christian Science Monitor's* John Hughes wrote from Saigon on July 2, "if fought by the Vietcong alone and unaided." French observers, who have stressed the NLF's jealous independence of both Hanoi and Peking, have made the same prediction. As we maximize our attacks, the Vietcong may have to retire to the jungles with their families. To exterminate them, the Pentagon reportedly estimates, could take ten years.

"Whatever the initial response from the other side," Sen. McGovern declares, ". . . the cessation of our bombing and {of} effective ground actions combined with a proposal for a cease-fire, open elections, and direct negotiations is the right policy for the United States. . . . it is the right policy even if the NLF rejects it for a time, because it will show the non-Communist political forces in Vietnam and the rest of the world that the United States desires peace and self-determination for Southeast Asia."

The President must choose for his own country, for both Vietnams, and for the peoples of Laos and Thailand, who are threatened by an expansion of the war.

The President, indeed, may be choosing for all mankind. His top advisers, Secretaries McNamara and Rusk, have admitted they cannot rule out the risk of war with China, and the Pentagon is known to have drawn up plans for nuclear warfare.

Of lesser magnitude, but still of importance, here at home, is the future of our good, if not our great, society. Sen. Fulbright warns:

> There is a kind of madness in the facile assumption that we can raise the many billions of dollars necessary to rebuild our schools and cities and

public transport and eliminate the pollution of air and water while also spending tens of billions to finance an 'open-ended' war in Asia, but even if the material resources can somehow be drawn from an expanding economy, I do not think that the spiritual resources will be forthcoming from an angry and disappointed people . . . When a nation is involved in a bitter foreign conflict, hopes give way to fears and creative and generous attitudes give way to a false and strident patriotism. . . .

"No one knows how long it will take . . . ." the President said at Omaha, "No one can tell you how much effort it will take. None can tell you how costly it will be . . . We will see this through; we shall persist; we shall succeed." The outcome of the war in Vietnam, he insisted, "will determine whether might makes right." He alone as our elected President must be trusted to decide how this country is to fulfill "its duty," how we are to be true to our "proud and glorious heritage."

Unpersuaded by the President's rhetoric, an increasing number of Americans are convinced we are not fulfilling our heritage, we are not being true to our belief in freedom for all peoples, and the United States itself is attempting to prove that might makes right.

Note at press time: On Aug. 24, the President told his press conference that the U.S. does not intend to maintain our bases and keep our men in South Vietnam and Thailand, and that "we are ready to stop the moment they {the North Vietnamese} are willing to stop." . . . A broadcast editorial in the Chinese Communist Party newspaper, *Jenminh Jih Pao,* reported from Tokyo on Aug. 30 by the *AP,* called for anti-American uprisings throughout the world—to nibble up U.S. imperialism. "By transferring the main weight of its forces to Asia," the editorial held, "U.S. imperialism is courting disaster." The paper charged the Soviet Union with working "energetically for a detente with Washington to freeze the situation in Europe," thus enabling the U.S. to concentrate its strength in Asia; and declared that the U.S., the Soviet Union, India and Japan "are working for the encirclement of China."

Bibliography

Alsop, Stewart, "His Business is War", *Saturday Evening Post.* May 21, 1966

American Friends Service Committee, *Peace in Vietnam,* New York: Hill and Wang, 1966

Bator, Victor, *Vietnam— A Diplomatic Tragedy,* Dobbs Ferry, N.Y.: Oceana Publications, Inc. 1965

Brightman, Carol, "The Geneva Agreements: Their Supervision and Control," *Viet-Report.* Oct. 1965

Browne, Robert S., "Vietnam Revisited," *Viet-Report.* Aug-Sept. 1965

Campbell, Alex, "Thailand—Is This Something to Fall Back On?" *New Republic,* Mch. 26, 1966

Carver, George A. Jr., "The Real Revolution in South Vietnam," *Foreign Affairs,* Apr. 1965

Devillers, Philippe, "Struggle for Unification of Vietnam," *China Quarterly,* Jan.-Mch. 1962

————*Histoire du Vietnam de 1940 à 1952* (3d ed) Paris: Editions du Seuil, 1952

————"Independence for Whom?" *Viet-Report,* Jan. 1966

Duncan, Donald, "'The Whole Thing Was a Lie'", *Ramparts,* Feb. 1966

Eisenhower, Dwight D. *Mandate for Change,* 1953-56. New York: Doubleday and Co., 1963

Fall, Bernard B. *The Two Viet-Nams: A Political and Military Analysis.* New York: Frederick A. Praeger, 1963, rev. 1964

————*Viet-Nam Witness 1953-66.* New York: Frederick A. Praeger, 1966

————"The Year of the Hawks," *The New York Times Magazine,* Dec. 12, 1965

————"'And Still the Little Men of the Vietcong Keep Coming'", *The New York Times Magazine,* Mch. 6, 1966

————and Marcus G. Raskin, Editors, *The Viet-Nam Reader*. Articles and Documents on American Foreign Policy and the Viet-Nam Crisis. New York: Vintage Books, 1965

Fulbright, J. William, *The Arrogance of Power*. Three lectures delivered at Johns Hopkins University, New York: Random House, 1966

Gettleman, Marvin E. Ed. *Vietnam: History, Documents and Opinions*. New York: Fawcett World Library, 1965

Geneva Conference: *Agreement on the Cessation of Hostilities in Vietnam* (July 20, 1954). *Final Declaration* (July 21, 1954), London: Great Britain Parliamentary Sessional Papers, XXXI (1953-54)

————*Interim Reports of the International Commission for Supervision and Control in Vietnam*. London: Great Britain Parliamentary Sessional Papers, Volumes XIX, XXX, XXXIII, XXXIX, XLV, and Command Paper 2069, (unbound)

Gigon, Fernand, *Les Americains face au Vietcong*, Paris: Flammarion, 1966

Goodwin, Richard N. *Triumph or Tragedy: Reflections on Vietnam*. New York: Random House, 1964

Graff, Henry F. "Teach-In on Vietnam By . . . The President, the Secretary of State, the Secretary of Defense and the Under Secretary of State", *The New York Times Magazine*, Mch. 20, 1966

Halberstam, David, *The Making of a Quagmire*, New York: Random House, 1964

Hammer, Ellen J., *The Struggle for Indochina* (Institute of Pacific Relations). Stanford, Cal.: Stanford University Press, 1954

I. F. Stone's Weekly

Kennedy, Sen. Edward, "A Fresh Look at Vietnam," *Look*, Feb. 8, 1966

Kraft, Joseph, *"Politics in Vietnam,"* New York Review of Books. June 23, 1966

Lacouture, Jean, *Vietnam: Between Two Truces,* New York: Random House, 1966; Vintage Books, 1966

————"Turning Point in Vietnam," *New York Review of Books,* Mch. 3, 1966

Lancaster, Donald, *The Emancipation of French Indochina,* London, New York, Toronto; Oxford University Press, 1961

Lansdale, Brig. Gen. Edward, "Vietnam: Do We Understand Revolution?" *Foreign Affairs,* Oct. 1964.

McDermott, John, "The History of Vietnam," in three parts, *Viet-Report,* I, June-Nov. 1965.

Morgenthau, Hans J. "Johnson's Dilemma—The Alternatives Now in Vietnam," *New Republic,* May 28, 1966

Ramparts, "Special Report on Southeast Asia," 1965

Ridgway, Gen. Matthew B. "Pull-Out, All-out, or Stand Fast in Vietnam?" *Look,* Apr. 5, 1966

Roberts, Chalmers M., "The Day We Didn't Go To War," *The Reporter,* Sept. 14, 1954

Sahlins, Marshall, "The Destruction of Conscience in Vietnam," *Dissent,* Jan.-Feb. 1966

Scheer, Robert, *How the United States Got Involved in Vietnam.* Santa Barbara, Cal.: Center for the Study of Democratic Institutions, 1965

Schlesinger, Arthur M., Jr. *A Thousand Days: John F. Kennedy in the White House,* Boston: The Houghton Mifflin Co., 1965

————"Vietnam?" *Look,* Aug. 9, 1966

Shaplen, Robert, *The Lost Revolution: The Story of Twenty Years of Neglected Opportunities in Vietnam and of America's Failure to Foster Democracy There,* New York: Harper and Row, 1965

————, "Letter from South Vietnam," *The New Yorker,* Mch. 12, 1966

Sevareid, Eric, "The Final Troubled Hours of Adlai Stevenson," *Look*, Nov. 30, 1965

Smith, Roger M., *Cambodia's Foreign Policy*, Ithaca, N.Y.: Cornell University Press, 1965

Tanham, George K., *Communist Revolutionary Warfare: The Vietminh in Indochina*, New York: Frederick A. Praeger, 1961

———— with W. Robert Warne, Earl J. Young, and William A. Nighswonger, *War Without Guns—American Civilians in Rural Vietnam*, New York: Praeger, 1966

Topping, Seymour, "Next on Peking's Hit Parade?" *The New York Times Magazine*, Feb. 20, 1966

U.S. Department of State, *Aggression from the North: The Record of North Vietnam's Campaign to Conquer South Vietnam*. The "White Paper" of Feb. 1965. U.S. Dept. of State Publication 7839: Far Eastern Series 130.

Vietnam Hearings, The. With an Introduction by J. William Fulbright, Chmn., U.S. Senate Committee on Foreign Relations. New York: Random House and Vintage Books, 1966

Warner, Denis, *The Last Confucian*, New York: The Macmillan Company, 1963

Zagoria, Donald S. "China's Crisis on Foreign Policy," *The New York Times Magazine*, May 1, 1966

Index